Better Homes and Gardens®

ALL-TIME FAVORITE *Salad* recipes

© 1978 by Meredith Corporation, Des Moines, Iowa.
All Rights Reserved. Printed in the United States of America.
Large-Format Edition. Third Printing, 1983.
Library of Congress Catalog Card Number: 77-085868
ISBN: 0-696-01130-1

On the cover: Salads add fresh flavor to any meal—*Crab-Stuffed Avocado* (see recipe, page 68), *Potato Salad Nicoise* (see recipe, page 25), and *Fruity Ginger Ale Mold* (see recipe, page 47).

BETTER HOMES AND GARDENS® BOOKS
Editor: Gerald Knox
Art Director: Ernest Shelton
Associate Art Director: Randall Yontz
Production and Copy Editors: Paul Kitzke,
   David Kirchner
Salad Cook Book Editors:
   Sally Pederson, Senior Food Editor
   Sandra Granseth, Senior Food Editor
Food Editor: Doris Eby
Senior Associate Food Editor: Sharyl Heiken
Senior Food Editor: Elizabeth Woolever
Associate Food Editors: Diane Nelson,
   Flora Szatkowski, Patricia Teberg
Salad Cook Book Designer:
   Sheryl Veenschoten
Senior Graphic Designer: Harijs Priekulis
Graphic Designers: Faith Berven,
   Richard Lewis, Neoma Alt West

Contents

SALAD FAVORITES

Add to your list of salad favorites from our wide collection of the best tasting and most popular recipes. These imaginative vegetable and fruit salads can introduce a dinner, serve as a tantalizing accompaniment to an entrée, or make up the main course for a satisfying but light meal. And you'll find the best of every variety featured in *Better Homes and Gardens All-Time Favorite Salad Recipes.*

Serve *Chef's Bowl* as a main dish salad (see recipe, page 60).

Waldorf Salad combines apples, celery, grapes, and nuts (see recipe, page 43).

Creamy Potato Salad is a hit all year round (see recipe, page 24).

Top *Salad Nicoise* (see recipe, page 14) with *Vinaigrette Dressing* (see recipe, page 85).

Colorful fruits and sweet dressings make a dazzling *Fruit Salad Platter* (page 41).

SIDE DISH SALADS

Round out your meals with fresh vegetable salads. You'll find easy-to-toss greens, home-style and potluck favorites, and vegetable-filled molded salads like these on the following pages: *Coleslaw Vinaigrette* (front, left), *Taos Salad Toss* (back, left), *Asparagus Toss* (front, right), and *Cucumber Ring Supreme* (back, right). (See index for recipe page numbers.)

Toss-it-together Greens

Spicy Italian Salad (pictured above)

- ½ **cup salad oil**
- ⅓ **cup tarragon vinegar**
- 1 **tablespoon sugar**
- 1 **teaspoon dried thyme, crushed**
- ½ **teaspoon dry mustard**
- 1 **small clove garlic, minced**
- 1 **7-ounce can artichoke hearts, drained and halved**
- 3 **cups torn romaine**
- 3 **cups torn iceberg lettuce**
- 1 **small sweet red *or* green pepper, cut in strips**
- ½ **cup chopped summer sausage**
- ¼ **cup sliced pitted ripe olives**
- 2 **tablespoons grated parmesan cheese**

In screw-top jar combine oil, vinegar, sugar, thyme, mustard, and garlic. Cover and shake well to mix. Pour over artichoke hearts. Cover; marinate in refrigerator 4 to 6 hours or overnight.

In salad bowl combine romaine, iceberg lettuce, red or green pepper, summer sausage, olives, and parmesan. Add artichokes with the dressing mixture. Toss to coat vegetables. Makes 6 servings.

Taos Salad Toss (pictured on page 6)

1 medium head iceberg
  lettuce, chopped
1 15-ounce can dark red
  kidney beans, drained
½ cup sliced pitted ripe
  olives
1 large avocado, mashed
½ cup dairy sour cream
¼ cup Italian salad dressing
1 tablespoon chopped canned
  green chili peppers
1 teaspoon minced dried
  onion
¾ teaspoon chili powder
¼ teaspoon salt
1 medium tomato, cut into
  wedges
½ cup shredded sharp cheddar
  cheese (2 ounces)
½ cup tortilla chips

In salad bowl combine lettuce, beans, and olives; chill. To make dressing, blend avocado and sour cream. Stir in Italian dressing, green chili peppers, onion, chili powder, salt, and dash *pepper;* mix well. Chill. Spoon avocado dressing in center of salad. Arrange tomato wedges in circle atop salad. Top with shredded cheese. Trim edge of bowl with tortilla chips. To serve, toss salad. Makes 8 servings.

Spring Salad Toss

3 cups torn iceberg lettuce
3 cups torn romaine
2 cups thinly sliced
  zucchini
½ cup sliced radishes
½ cup sliced fresh mushrooms
3 green onions, sliced
  Salt
  Pepper
  Italian salad dressing
½ cup crumbled blue cheese

In large salad bowl combine lettuce, romaine, zucchini, radishes, mushrooms, and green onions. Season with salt and pepper. Toss lightly with Italian dressing to coat vegetables; sprinkle blue cheese atop. Makes 6 servings.

Marinated Vegetable Salad

2 cups thinly sliced
  cucumber
2 cups thinly sliced carrot
1 medium onion, sliced and
  separated into rings
½ cup chopped celery
1 cup vinegar
¾ cup sugar
¼ cup salad oil
1 teaspoon celery seed
1 teaspoon salt
¼ teaspoon pepper
  Lettuce

In large bowl combine cucumber, carrot, onion, and celery. To make dressing, in screw-top jar combine vinegar, sugar, salad oil, celery seed, salt, and pepper. Cover and shake to mix well. Pour over vegetables; stir gently. Cover and refrigerate several hours or overnight, stirring occasionally.

To serve, drain the vegetables, reserving marinade. Mound vegetables in lettuce-lined bowl. Return any leftover vegetables to marinade; store in refrigerator. Makes 6 to 8 servings.

Raw Vegetable Antipasto (opposite, above)

1 tomato, peeled and thinly
  sliced
1 cup cauliflowerets
1 cup broccoli buds
1 cucumber, sliced
1 zucchini, cut into sticks
1 carrot, cut into sticks
1 onion slice, separated
  into rings
½ cup olive oil
3 tablespoons wine vinegar
1 teaspoon dried oregano,
  crushed
½ teaspoon salt
¼ teaspoon pepper
  Bibb lettuce leaves
½ cup pitted ripe olives

In shallow dish combine tomato, cauliflowerets, broccoli, cucumber, zucchini, carrot, and onion rings. To make dressing, in screw-top jar combine olive oil, wine vinegar, oregano, salt, and pepper. Cover and shake to mix well. Pour dressing over the vegetables in dish. Cover and refrigerate 2 to 3 hours, spooning dressing over vegetables occasionally. Drain. Arrange vegetables on lettuce-lined platter. Garnish the center of the salad with ripe olives. Makes about 8 to 10 appetizer servings or 4 to 6 salad servings.

Tomatoes Rosé (opposite, below left)

4 large tomatoes, peeled and
  thinly sliced
½ cup rosé wine
⅓ cup salad oil
3 tablespoons wine vinegar
¼ cup finely chopped celery
¼ cup thinly sliced green onion
1 envelope Italian salad
  dressing mix
  Celery leaves

Place tomatoes in shallow dish or deep bowl. To make dressing, in screw-top jar combine wine, salad oil, and vinegar. Stir in celery, green onion, and dressing mix. Cover and shake to mix well. Pour dressing over tomatoes. Cover; refrigerate several hours. Lift tomatoes from marinade. Arrange slices of tomato on platter. Spoon some of the dressing over; pass remaining. Garnish with celery leaves. Makes 6 servings.

Broccoli Vinaigrette (opposite, below right)

1 pound fresh broccoli *or*
  2 10-ounce packages
  frozen broccoli spears
¾ cup Vinaigrette Dressing
  (see recipe, page 85)
⅓ cup finely chopped dill
  pickle
⅓ cup finely chopped green
  pepper
3 tablespoons snipped
  parsley
2 tablespoons capers,
  drained
1 hard-cooked egg, finely
  chopped

Cut fresh broccoli stalks lengthwise into uniform spears, following branching lines. Cook fresh broccoli in small amount of boiling salted water 10 to 15 minutes, frozen broccoli 4 to 5 minutes, or just till crisp-tender. Drain. In screw-top jar combine *Vinaigrette Dressing*, dill pickle, chopped green pepper, snipped parsley, and capers. Cover and shake to mix well. Pour dressing over broccoli spears; refrigerate several hours or overnight. Drain off liquid. Arrange broccoli spears on serving plate; top with finely chopped egg. Garnish with additional sawtooth-cut, hard-cooked eggs filled with sieved egg yolks, if desired. Makes 6 to 8 servings.

Serve fresh-tasting *Raw Vegetable Antipasto* for pre-dinner snacking.
You can forget the plates and forks with a pick-up-and-munch assortment like this.

Italian salad dressing mix and wine
make the flavorful marinade for *Tomatoes Rosé*.

Dress up *Broccoli Vinaigrette*
with a fancy stuffed egg garnish.

The secret to the taste of *24-Hour Vegetable Salad* is allowing the flavors time to blend.

Garden Row Salad goes together in a jiffy, with help from your blender or food processor.

Raw cauliflower and zucchini add crunch to *Forgotten Four-Layer Salad*.

24-Hour Vegetable Salad (opposite, above)

1 head iceberg lettuce, torn
  Sugar
6 hard-cooked eggs, sliced
1 10-ounce package frozen
  peas, thawed
1 pound bacon, crisp-cooked,
  drained, and crumbled
2 cups shredded Swiss cheese
1 cup mayonnaise *or* salad
  dressing

In bottom of large bowl place *3 cups* of the lettuce; sprinkle with a little sugar, *salt*, and *pepper*. Layer eggs atop lettuce in bowl, standing some eggs on edge, if desired. Sprinkle generously with *salt*. Next, layer in order: peas, remaining lettuce, bacon, and cheese. Spread mayonnaise or salad dressing over top, sealing to edge of bowl. Cover and refrigerate 24 hours or overnight. Garnish with sliced green onion and paprika, if desired. Toss before serving. Makes 12 to 15 servings.

Garden Row Salad (opposite, below left)

3 medium carrots, cut up
1 large cucumber, halved,
  seeded, and cut up
4 stalks celery, cut up
1 pint cherry tomatoes,
  halved
1 cup cubed sharp cheddar
  cheese (4 ounces)
½ slice bread, torn
1½ cups Garlic Croutons
  (see recipe, page 91)
2 hard-cooked eggs, sliced
6 slices bacon, crisp-cooked,
  drained, and crumbled
  Russian Dressing (see
  recipe, page 83)

Put carrots in blender container; cover with *cold* water. Cover with lid and blend till coarsely chopped. Drain and set aside. Repeat process with cucumber, then celery.

In salad bowl layer chopped carrots, cucumber, cherry tomato halves, and celery. Cover and chill. Wipe blender container dry. Combine cheese and bread in blender container; cover and blend till coarsely chopped.

Just before serving, arrange cheese mixture, *Garlic Croutons*, egg slices, and bacon atop salad. To serve, toss with *Russian Dressing*. Makes 10 to 12 servings.

Note: To prepare salad in a food processor, cut carrots, cucumber, and celery into chunks. Put through coarse shredding blade of food processor. Cut cheese into chunks and put through coarse shredding blade along with bread pieces.

Forgotten Four-Layer Salad (opposite, below right)

1 head iceberg lettuce, torn
2 cups thinly sliced
  cauliflowerets
2 cups thinly sliced zucchini
1 small red onion, sliced
  and separated into rings
⅓ cup mayonnaise *or* salad
  dressing
⅓ cup creamy French salad
  dressing
1 tablespoon lemon juice
1 tablespoon prepared
  horseradish
1 teaspoon worcestershire
  sauce
4 to 6 drops bottled hot
  pepper sauce
½ cup frozen whipped dessert
  topping, thawed

In salad bowl layer lettuce, cauliflowerets, zucchini, and onion. To make dressing, in mixing bowl stir together mayonnaise or salad dressing, French dressing, lemon juice, horseradish, worcestershire, and hot pepper sauce. Fold in whipped topping. Spoon dressing over vegetables in bowl. Sprinkle with paprika, if desired. Cover and refrigerate 4 to 6 hours or overnight. Toss just before serving. Makes 8 servings.

Salad Nicoise (opposite, above)

3 cups torn romaine
1 head bibb lettuce, torn
   (2 cups)
1 7-ounce can water-pack
   tuna, drained
1 10-ounce package frozen
   cut green beans, cooked,
   drained, and chilled
1 cup cherry tomatoes,
   halved
1 small green pepper, cut
   into rings
1 small onion, sliced and
   separated into rings
3 hard-cooked eggs, cut
   into wedges
1 medium potato, cooked,
   chilled, and sliced
½ cup pitted ripe olives
1 2-ounce can anchovy
   fillets, drained
¾ cup Vinaigrette Dressing
   (see recipe, page 85)

Line large platter with torn romaine and bibb lettuce. Break tuna into chunks; mound in center of torn lettuce. Arrange chilled green beans, tomatoes, green pepper, onion rings, egg wedges, potato, olives, and anchovy fillets atop the lettuce. Cover and chill. Just before serving, drizzle with *Vinaigrette Dressing;* toss. Makes 6 to 8 servings.

Caesar Salad (opposite, below)

1 egg
1 clove garlic, halved
3 anchovy fillets
3 tablespoons olive oil
½ lemon
   **Few dashes worcestershire
   sauce**
6 cups torn romaine
¼ cup grated parmesan cheese
½ cup Garlic Croutons (see
   recipe, page 91)
   Freshly ground pepper

Allow egg to come to room temperature. To coddle egg, place whole egg in small saucepan of boiling water; remove from heat and let stand 1 minute. Cool slightly. Rub large wooden salad bowl with cut garlic clove; discard garlic. In bottom of bowl combine anchovy fillets and olive oil. Using a fork or the back of a spoon, mash till smooth. Squeeze lemon over the mixture; blend in worcestershire. Break the coddled egg into the bowl and mix till dressing becomes creamy. Add romaine; toss to coat. Sprinkle with parmesan, *Garlic Croutons*, and pepper; toss gently to mix. Makes 6 servings.

Preparing Salad Greens

To prepare lettuce for use, remove and discard wilted outer leaves. For thorough rinsing, remove core from head lettuce; separate leafy lettuce. Rinse the greens in cold water. Drain. Place leafy greens in clean kitchen towel or paper toweling, and pat or toss gently to remove clinging water. Tear greens into bite-size pieces. (Tearing exposes the interior and allows dressing to be absorbed by the greens.) Place greens in salad bowl; cover with damp paper towel and refrigerate until serving time.

French *Salad Niçoise* originated in Nice in the heart of the Provençal cooking region. Tuna, potatoes, green beans, tomatoes, and hard-cooked eggs are all tossed with *Vinaigrette Dressing.*

Famous *Caesar Salad* was created by an innovative restaurateur. Though the technique and ingredients vary slightly from chef to chef, the tossing always is done tableside with great flair and flourish.

Asparagus Toss (pictured on page 7)

1 pound fresh asparagus,
  cut into 2-inch pieces
  (2 cups)
½ cup salad oil
¼ cup finely chopped
  canned beets
2 tablespoons white wine
  vinegar
2 tablespoons lemon juice
1 teaspoon sugar
1 teaspoon salt
1 teaspoon paprika
½ teaspoon dry mustard
4 drops bottled hot pepper
  sauce
5 cups torn iceberg lettuce
1 cup sliced celery
1 hard-cooked egg, chopped
¼ cup sliced green onion

Cook asparagus in boiling salted water 8 to 10 minutes or till just tender; drain. Chill.

To make dressing, in screw-top jar combine salad oil, beets, vinegar, lemon juice, sugar, salt, paprika, dry mustard, and hot pepper sauce. Cover and shake well to mix. Chill. In salad bowl combine chilled asparagus, lettuce, celery, egg, and green onion. Pour dressing over salad. Toss to coat vegetables. Garnish salad with additional sliced canned beets, if desired. Makes 6 servings.

South American Mixed Salad

1 medium cucumber, peeled
2 large bananas, sliced
2 sweet red *or* green peppers,
  cut in thin strips
1 avocado, seeded, peeled,
  and sliced
½ small onion, sliced and
  separated into rings
⅓ cup vinegar
¼ cup olive *or* salad oil
½ teaspoon salt
¼ teaspoon bottled hot
  pepper sauce

Halve cucumber lengthwise; remove seeds and slice crosswise. Arrange cucumber, bananas, peppers, avocado, and onion in salad bowl. To make dressing, in screw-top jar combine vinegar, oil, salt, and bottled hot pepper sauce. Cover and shake to mix well. Pour dressing over vegetable mixture; toss to coat. Cover and refrigerate 1 to 2 hours. Makes 8 servings.

Mushroom-Avocado Duo

½ cup salad oil
3 tablespoons tarragon
  vinegar
2 tablespoons lemon juice
2 tablespoons water
1 tablespoon snipped
  parsley
1 clove garlic, minced
¾ teaspoon salt
8 ounces fresh mushrooms,
  halved (3 cups)
2 avocados, seeded, peeled,
  and sliced

To make dressing, in screw-top jar combine salad oil, tarragon vinegar, lemon juice, water, snipped parsley, minced garlic, salt, and a dash *pepper*. Cover and shake well to mix. Pour dressing over mushrooms and avocados in shallow dish. Cover and refrigerate several hours; occasionally spoon over dressing. To serve, drain mushrooms and avocados and arrange on serving platter. Garnish with parsley sprigs, if desired. Makes 8 servings.

Spinach-Mushroom Salad

1 small clove garlic, halved
4 cups torn fresh spinach
1 cup sliced fresh mushrooms
2 hard-cooked eggs, sliced
¼ cup salad oil
2 tablespoons lemon juice
¼ teaspoon salt

Rub wooden salad bowl with cut garlic clove; discard garlic. In bowl combine spinach, mushrooms, and sliced eggs. Cover and chill.

To make dressing, in screw-top jar combine salad oil, lemon juice, salt, and a few dashes freshly ground *pepper*. Cover and shake to mix well. Chill. Pour over salad just before serving; toss to coat vegetables. Makes 4 to 6 servings.

Wilted Spinach Salad

5 slices bacon, cut up
½ cup sliced green onion
2 tablespoons white wine vinegar
1 tablespoon lemon juice
2 teaspoons sugar
½ teaspoon salt
8 cups torn fresh spinach
   (1 pound)
1 hard-cooked egg, chopped

In large skillet cook bacon over medium heat till crisp. Add green onion, vinegar, lemon juice, sugar, salt, and a few dashes freshly ground *pepper*. Gradually add spinach, tossing only until leaves are coated and wilted slightly. Turn into salad bowl. Sprinkle with chopped egg. Makes 4 servings.

Tossed Mixed Greens

3 cups torn iceberg lettuce
2 cups torn fresh spinach
1 cup watercress leaves
1 medium tomato, cut in wedges
¼ cup chopped celery
1 tablespoon snipped chives
¼ cup sugar
¼ cup white wine vinegar
1 tablespoon finely chopped
   onion
½ teaspoon dry mustard
¼ teaspoon salt
¼ teaspoon worcestershire
   sauce
   Few drops bottled hot
   pepper sauce
⅓ cup salad oil

In salad bowl combine lettuce, spinach, watercress, tomato wedges, celery, and chives. To make dressing, in small mixer bowl combine sugar and white wine vinegar; blend in onion, dry mustard, salt, worcestershire sauce, and bottled hot pepper sauce. Gradually add salad oil, beating with electric mixer about 2 minutes or till thick. Cover and chill. Pour dressing over salad. Toss to coat vegetables. Makes 6 servings.

Fresh Spinach Tips

Choose fresh spinach with large green leaves; avoid yellowed leaves. Store unwashed spinach, loosely covered, in the vegetable crisper of the refrigerator. For best flavor, plan to use the spinach within a few days. Before using spinach, rinse leaves in lukewarm water to remove sand. Remove and discard stems. Pat leaves dry with paper toweling.

Enjoy the sophisticated taste of anchovy-topped *Greek Salad*. Cubes of
sharp feta cheese and an herb, vinegar, and oil dressing blend for a distinctive flavor.

Greek Salad (opposite)

1 medium head iceberg
   lettuce, chopped
1 head curly endive, chopped
2 tomatoes, peeled and
   chopped (1 cup)
¾ cup cubed feta cheese
   (3 ounces)
¼ cup sliced pitted
   ripe olives
¼ cup sliced green onion
1 2-ounce can anchovy
   fillets, drained
⅔ cup olive or salad oil
⅓ cup white wine vinegar
¼ teaspoon dried oregano,
   crushed

In mixing bowl toss together chopped lettuce and endive; mound onto 6 individual salad plates. Atop greens arrange tomatoes, feta cheese, olives, green onion, and anchovies. To make dressing, in screw-top jar combine oil, vinegar, oregano, ½ teaspoon *salt,* and ⅛ teaspoon *pepper.* Cover and shake well to mix. Pour dressing over salads. Makes 6 servings.

Belgian Tossed Salad

1 10-ounce package frozen
   brussels sprouts
½ cup salad oil
⅓ cup vinegar
1 clove garlic, minced
1 teaspoon dried parsley
   flakes, crushed
¼ teaspoon dried basil,
   crushed
8 cups torn mixed salad
   greens
½ medium red onion, sliced
   and separated into rings
6 slices bacon, crisp-cooked,
   drained, and crumbled

Cook brussels sprouts in small amount of boiling salted water about 5 minutes or till barely tender; drain. To make dressing, in screw-top jar combine oil, vinegar, garlic, parsley, basil, ½ teaspoon *salt,* and ⅛ teaspoon *pepper.* Cover and shake well to mix. Cut brussels sprouts in half lengthwise; pour dressing over. Cover; chill 3 to 4 hours.

In salad bowl combine greens, onion rings, and bacon. Add brussels sprouts with dressing; toss to coat vegetables. Makes 8 servings.

Oriental Garden Toss

6 ounces fresh pea pods or
   1 6-ounce package
   frozen pea pods, thawed
½ cup salad oil
⅓ cup vinegar
2 tablespoons sugar
1 tablespoon soy sauce
¼ teaspoon ground ginger
4 cups sliced Chinese
   cabbage
4 cups torn leaf lettuce
1 cup fresh bean sprouts
2 tablespoons chopped
   pimiento

Trim ends from fresh pea pods. Cook pea pods in 2 cups of boiling salted water for 1 minute; drain well. To make dressing, in screw-top jar combine salad oil, vinegar, sugar, soy sauce, ginger, ½ teaspoon *salt,* and ⅛ teaspoon freshly ground *pepper.* Cover and shake well to mix. Pour dressing over pea pods; cover and refrigerate 1 to 2 hours. In large salad bowl combine Chinese cabbage, leaf lettuce, bean sprouts, and pimiento. Add pea pods and dressing. Toss to coat vegetables. Makes 6 to 8 servings.

Bermuda Salad Bowl (opposite, above)

1 small head cauliflower,
  broken into flowerets
½ large bermuda onion,
  sliced and separated
  into rings
½ cup sliced pimiento-
  stuffed olives
⅔ cup French salad dressing
1 small head iceberg lettuce,
  torn (4 cups)
½ cup crumbled blue cheese
  (2 ounces)

Slice the flowerets. In large salad bowl combine cauliflower, onion rings, and olives. Pour French dressing over salad. Toss to coat vegetables. Cover and refrigerate 30 minutes. Just before serving, add the lettuce and blue cheese; toss lightly. Pass extra French dressing, if desired. Makes 8 to 10 servings.

Curried Vegetable Salad (opposite, below)

3 medium turnips, peeled,
  halved, and thinly
  sliced
3 medium carrots, sliced
½ small head cauliflower, broken
  into flowerets
1 medium green pepper, cut
  in strips
½ cup vinegar
⅓ cup sugar
¼ cup salad oil
2 teaspoons curry powder
1 teaspoon salt
⅛ teaspoon pepper
  Romaine (optional)

In covered saucepan cook turnips, carrots, cauliflowerets, and green pepper in small amount boiling salted water about 5 minutes or till crisp-tender. Drain and cool. To make dressing, in screw-top jar combine vinegar, sugar, salad oil, curry powder, salt, and pepper. Cover and shake to mix well. Pour curry dressing over vegetables. Toss to coat vegetables. Cover and refrigerate 4 hours or overnight, stirring occasionally. To serve, lift vegetables from dressing with a slotted spoon. Serve in romaine-lined bowl, if desired. Makes 8 servings.

Piquant Cauliflower

1 medium head cauliflower,
  broken into flowerets
1 cup cherry tomatoes,
  halved
½ cup salad oil
⅓ cup vinegar
2 tablespoons sliced
  pimiento-stuffed
  olives
1 tablespoon sweet pickle
  relish
1 teaspoon sugar
1 teaspoon paprika
½ teaspoon salt
⅛ teaspoon pepper
  Lettuce

In covered saucepan cook cauliflowerets in small amount of boiling salted water 9 to 10 minutes or till crisp-tender. Drain. In deep bowl combine cauliflowerets and tomatoes. To make dressing, in screw-top jar combine salad oil, vinegar, olives, pickle relish, sugar, paprika, salt, and pepper. Cover and shake to mix well. Pour dressing over cauliflower and tomatoes. Cover and refrigerate 2 to 3 hours, stirring occasionally. To serve, lift vegetables from dressing with slotted spoon. Serve in lettuce-lined bowl. Makes 8 servings.

Deep red onion rings are the center of attention in this unusual combination of vegetables. Pour on bottled French dressing and spark *Bermuda Salad Bowl* with chunks of crumbled blue cheese.

Marinate part of your fall garden harvest in a zesty curry dressing. Make up a big batch— you can store *Curried Vegetable Salad* in the refrigerator and enjoy encores for up to one week.

Hearts of Palm Salad

2 tablespoons vinegar
⅛ teaspoon dried tarragon, crushed
⅛ teaspoon dried thyme, crushed
⅛ teaspoon dried basil, crushed
⅓ cup olive *or* salad oil
1 tablespoon dijon-style mustard
1 clove garlic, minced
½ teaspoon salt
½ teaspoon pepper
1 14-ounce can hearts of palm, drained
6 cups torn mixed salad greens
1 medium tomato, cut in wedges (optional)

To make dressing, in screw-top jar combine vinegar, tarragon, thyme, and basil; let stand for 1 hour. Add olive or salad oil, mustard, garlic, salt, and pepper. Shake well to mix. Cover and chill.

Cut hearts of palm into bite-size pieces. In large salad bowl combine hearts of palm and torn greens. Pour dressing over salad. Toss to coat vegetables. Garnish with tomato wedges, if desired. Makes 6 servings.

Sweet-Sour Swiss Chard

6 cups torn Swiss chard
6 slices bacon
½ cup sliced green onion
4 teaspoons sugar
2 teaspoons all-purpose flour
½ teaspoon salt
⅓ cup water
¼ cup vinegar

Place torn chard leaves in large salad bowl; set aside. In skillet cook bacon till crisp. Drain bacon, reserving ¼ cup of the bacon drippings. Crumble bacon and set aside. In same skillet cook onion in reserved drippings over low heat till tender but not brown. Blend in sugar, flour, and salt; stir in water and vinegar. Cook and stir till thick and bubbly. Pour hot mixture over chard, tossing to coat leaves. Sprinkle with crumbled bacon. Serve immediately. Makes 4 to 6 servings.

Zucchini Salad

1 cup white wine vinegar
⅔ cup olive oil
2 tablespoons sugar
1 clove garlic, minced
1 teaspoon salt
1 teaspoon dried basil, crushed
Few dashes pepper
4 cups sliced zucchini
Leaf lettuce
¼ cup sliced green onion
2 medium tomatoes, cut in thin wedges

To make dressing, in screw-top jar combine white wine vinegar, olive oil, sugar, garlic, salt, basil, and pepper. Cover and shake to mix well. Cook sliced zucchini in small amount of boiling salted water about 3 minutes or till crisp-tender. Drain. Arrange *half* the zucchini in single layer in 10×6×2-inch dish. Shake dressing; pour *half* over zucchini. Arrange remaining zucchini over first layer. Pour on remaining dressing. Cover and refrigerate several hours or overnight. To serve, drain zucchini, reserving ¼ cup dressing. Arrange zucchini on a lettuce-lined plate; top with sliced green onion. Arrange tomato wedges around zucchini; drizzle with the reserved dressing. Makes 8 servings.

Tomato-Cucumber Salad

2 tomatoes, cut into wedges
1 cucumber, scored and
   sliced
¼ cup pitted ripe olives
¼ cup salad oil
3 tablespoons lemon juice
½ teaspoon salt
¼ teaspoon dry mustard
⅛ teaspoon garlic powder
  Freshly ground pepper
  Leaf lettuce (optional)

In bowl combine tomato wedges, sliced cucumber, and olives. To make dressing, in screw-top jar combine salad oil, lemon juice, salt, dry mustard, garlic powder, and pepper. Cover and shake well to mix. Pour dressing over vegetables. Cover and refrigerate several hours, spooning dressing over vegetables occasionally. Lift vegetables from dressing with slotted spoon. Serve on lettuce leaves, if desired. Makes 4 servings.

Marinated Relish Salad

1 16-ounce can bean sprouts,
   rinsed and drained
2 cups sliced fresh
   mushrooms
2 cups sliced cauliflower
1 medium cucumber, peeled
   and sliced
1 medium green pepper, cut
   in strips
⅓ cup sliced green onion
1⅓ cups vinegar
½ cup sugar
⅓ cup salad oil
1 clove garlic, minced
½ teaspoon salt
12 cherry tomatoes, halved

Combine bean sprouts, mushrooms, cauliflower, cucumber, green pepper, and onion. To make dressing, in screw-top jar combine vinegar, sugar, salad oil, garlic, and salt. Cover and shake well to mix. Pour dressing over vegetables. Toss to coat vegetables. Cover and refrigerate several hours or overnight. To serve, add cherry tomatoes; toss lightly. Makes 12 to 14 servings.

Spinach-Apple Toss

½ cup salad oil
¼ cup lemon juice
1 tablespoon sliced green onion
1 teaspoon sugar
½ teaspoon dried mint, crushed,
   or 1 tablespoon fresh mint,
   chopped
10 ounces fresh spinach, torn
   (about 8 cups)
2 medium apples, cored
   thinly sliced
1 small cucumber, thinly sliced
⅓ cup sliced radishes
2 tablespoons shelled sunflower
   seed

In a screw-top jar combine oil, lemon juice, onion, sugar, mint, ½ teaspoon *salt,* and dash *pepper.* Cover; shake well. Chill. In a large salad bowl combine spinach, sliced apple, cucumber, radishes, and sunflower seed. Shake dressing; pour over salad. Toss to coat. Makes 8 to 10 servings.

Home-style Salads

Creamy Potato Salad (pictured above)

- 1 tablespoon sugar
- 2 teaspoons all-purpose flour
- 1½ teaspoons dry mustard
- ¾ teaspoon salt
- 3 slightly beaten egg yolks
- ¾ cup milk
- ¼ cup vinegar
- 3 tablespoons butter *or* margarine
- 1 cup whipping cream
- 9 medium potatoes (3 pounds)
- 1 cup chopped celery
- ⅓ cup sliced green onion
- ¼ cup sweet pickle relish
- 1½ teaspoons salt
- ⅛ teaspoon pepper
- ½ cup sliced radishes
- Hard-cooked egg slices
- Parsley sprig

To make dressing, in saucepan combine sugar, flour, mustard, and the ¾ teaspoon salt. Add egg yolks and milk. Cook and stir over low heat till thickened. *(Do not boil.)* Blend in vinegar and butter or margarine. Cool. Whip cream to soft peaks; fold into cooked mixture.

Meanwhile, in covered saucepan cook potatoes in boiling salted water for 25 to 30 minutes or till tender; drain. Cool slightly. Peel and slice potatoes. In large bowl combine potatoes, celery, green onion, relish, 1½ teaspoons salt, and pepper. Stir in the cooked dressing. Toss lightly to coat vegetables. Cover and chill. Before serving, fold in radishes. Garnish with egg slices and parsley. Makes 12 to 16 servings.

Potato Salad Nicoise (pictured on the cover)

Vinaigrette Dressing (see recipe, page 85)
4 medium potatoes (1½ pounds)
1 7-ounce can artichoke hearts, drained and halved
1 small red onion, sliced and separated into rings
1 small green pepper, sliced into thin rings
1 cup cherry tomatoes
¼ cup pitted ripe olives
Leaf lettuce
3 hard-cooked eggs, quartered
1 2-ounce can anchovy fillets, drained
¼ cup snipped parsley

Prepare *Vinaigrette Dressing*. In covered saucepan cook potatoes in boiling salted water for 25 to 30 minutes or till tender; drain. Peel and cube potatoes. Combine potatoes, artichokes, onion rings, green pepper, tomatoes, and olives; toss with dressing. Cover and chill several hours or overnight, stirring gently once or twice. To assemble salad, drain dressing from potato mixture; reserve dressing. Line salad bowl with lettuce. Spoon potato mixture onto lettuce. Arrange hard-cooked eggs and anchovies on top. Sprinkle with snipped parsley. Pass the reserved dressing. Makes 8 to 10 servings.

German Potato Salad

6 medium potatoes (2 pounds)
6 slices bacon
½ cup chopped onion
2 tablespoons all-purpose flour
2 tablespoons sugar
1½ teaspoons salt
1 teaspoon celery seed
Dash pepper
1 cup water
½ cup vinegar
2 hard-cooked eggs, sliced

In covered saucepan cook potatoes in boiling salted water for 25 to 30 minutes or till tender; drain. Peel and slice potatoes. In large skillet cook bacon till crisp; drain and crumble, reserving ¼ cup drippings. Cook onion in the reserved drippings till tender but not brown. Blend in flour, sugar, salt, celery seed, and pepper. Add water and vinegar. Cook and stir till thickened. Stir in bacon and potatoes. Cook about 5 minutes or till heated through, tossing lightly. Add hard-cooked eggs; toss lightly just to mix vegetables. Makes 6 to 8 servings.

Potluck Potato Salad

3 tablespoons vinegar
2 teaspoons mustard seed
1½ teaspoons celery seed
9 medium potatoes (3 pounds)
1 cup chopped celery
½ cup thinly sliced green onion
3 hard-cooked eggs, chopped
2 cups mayonnaise *or* salad dressing
1 teaspoon salt
Paprika

Combine vinegar, mustard seed, and celery seed; let stand several hours. In covered saucepan cook potatoes in boiling salted water for 25 to 30 minutes or till tender; drain. Peel and cube potatoes. In large bowl sprinkle potatoes with a little salt. Add celery, onion, and eggs; toss lightly. Combine mayonnaise, salt, and vinegar mixture. Add to potato mixture; toss to mix vegetables. Chill. Sprinkle with paprika. Makes 12 to 15 servings.

Bean and Carrot Salad (opposite, above)

1 16-ounce can (2 cups) cut
    green beans, drained
1 16-ounce can (2 cups)
    sliced carrots, drained
1 15½-ounce can (2 cups) red
    kidney beans, drained
1 small onion, thinly sliced
¼ cup chopped green pepper
¼ cup chopped celery
2 tablespoons snipped parsley
½ cup vinegar
⅓ cup sugar
2 tablespoons salad oil
1 teaspoon dry mustard
    Dash pepper

In deep bowl combine green beans, carrots, kidney beans, onion, green pepper, celery, and parsley. In a screw-top jar combine vinegar, sugar, oil, mustard, and pepper; cover and shake well to mix. Pour mixture over vegetables and stir to coat. Cover and refrigerate several hours or overnight, stirring occasionally. To serve, spoon vegetables into serving dish, arranging onion rings atop. Makes 10 to 12 servings.

Scandinavian Cucumbers (opposite, below right)

½ cup dairy sour cream
2 tablespoons snipped parsley
2 tablespoons tarragon vinegar
1 tablespoon sugar
1 tablespoon snipped chives
3 small unpeeled cucumbers,
    thinly sliced (3 cups)

Stir together sour cream, parsley, tarragon vinegar, sugar, and chives. Gently fold in cucumbers. Cover and chill. Makes 6 servings.

Dilly Macaroni Salad (opposite, below left)

1 cup elbow macaroni
1 cup cubed American cheese
    (4 ounces)
½ cup sliced celery
½ cup chopped green pepper
3 tablespoons chopped
    pimiento
½ cup mayonnaise *or* salad
    dressing
1 tablespoon vinegar
¾ teaspoon salt
½ teaspoon dried dillweed

Cook macaroni according to package directions; drain well. Cool. Combine macaroni, cheese cubes, celery, green pepper, and pimiento.

    Blend together mayonnaise or salad dressing, vinegar, salt, and dillweed; add to macaroni mixture. Toss lightly. Cover and chill well. Serve salad in lettuce-lined bowl, if desired. Makes 6 servings.

Toting Picnic Salads

To keep salads chilled for patio buffets or summer picnic outings, pack cold prepared salads in an insulated ice bucket. Secure lid with masking tape. The container is easy to tote and doubles as an attractive serving dish.

Bean and Carrot Salad provides a refreshing twist to the popular
three-bean salad. A deviled dressing complements the colorful vegetable combination.

A sprinkling of dillweed gives
Dilly Macaroni Salad a summer-fresh taste.

Seasoned sour cream accents the
crisp vegetable in *Scandinavian Cucumbers*.

You're sure to find your favorite coleslaw among this cabbage-patch selection.
For *Tangy Coleslaw*, toss red and green cabbage with a spunky, home-cooked dressing.

Tangy Coleslaw (pictured above)

    1 tablespoon butter *or*
      margarine
    4 teaspoons all-purpose flour
    2 tablespoons sugar
    1 teaspoon dry mustard
    ½ teaspoon salt
      Dash white pepper
  1½ cups milk
    ⅓ cup vinegar
    2 tablespoons lemon juice
    3 cups shredded green cabbage
    1 cup shredded red cabbage
    1 cup shredded carrot
    ¼ cup chopped green pepper

In saucepan melt butter over low heat. Blend in flour, sugar, mustard, salt, and white pepper. Add milk; cook and stir till thickened and bubbly. Stir in vinegar and lemon juice. Chill. Combine cabbages, carrot, and green pepper. Pour chilled dressing over vegetables; toss to coat vegetables. Garnish with carrot curls, if desired. Makes 6 to 8 servings.

Coleslaw Vinaigrette (pictured on page 6)

2 cups shredded cabbage
⅓ cup sliced green onion
¼ cup snipped parsley
3 tablespoons vinegar
2 tablespoons sugar
2 tablespoons salad oil
1 teaspoon salt
2 hard-cooked eggs, chilled

Combine cabbage, onion, and parsley. Stir together vinegar, sugar, salad oil, and salt till sugar is dissolved. Pour vinegar mixture over vegetables; toss to coat vegetables. Cover and chill. Separate yolk from white of one hard-cooked egg. Cut up white; toss with cabbage. Slice remaining egg; arrange atop salad. Sieve yolk over the egg slices. Makes 4 servings.

Crunchy Garden Slaw

4 cups finely shredded
   cabbage
1 cup thinly sliced celery
1 cup chopped cucumber
½ cup chopped green pepper
½ cup mayonnaise or salad
   dressing
2 tablespoons vinegar
1 teaspoon prepared mustard
½ teaspoon sugar
¼ teaspoon salt
¼ teaspoon paprika
1 tablespoon chopped
   pimiento

Combine shredded cabbage, celery, cucumber, and green pepper. Stir together mayonnaise or salad dressing, vinegar, mustard, sugar, salt, and paprika. Pour mayonnaise mixture over vegetables; toss to coat vegetables. Cover and chill. Garnish with pimiento. Makes 8 servings.

Cabbage to Coleslaw

To make coleslaw the way you like it, follow these guides for cutting cabbage. (A) For long, coarse shreds, hold quarter head of cabbage firmly against cutting surface; slice with long-bladed knife. (B) For short, medium shreds, push quarter head of cabbage across coarse blade of vegetable shredder. (C) For fine, juicy shreds, cut cabbage into small wedges. Place half the wedges at a time in blender container; cover with cold water. Blend till chopped. Drain.

Macaroni-Cheddar Salad

3 cups medium shell macaroni
  (10 ounces)
1 cup dairy sour cream
1 cup mayonnaise *or* salad
  dressing
¼ cup milk
½ cup sweet pickle relish
2 tablespoons vinegar
2 teaspoons prepared mustard
¾ teaspoon salt
2 cups cubed cheddar cheese
  (8 ounces)
1 cup chopped celery
½ cup chopped green pepper
¼ cup chopped onion

Cook macaroni according to package directions; drain. Rinse with cold water. Drain and set aside. Combine sour cream, mayonnaise, and milk; stir in pickle relish, vinegar, mustard, and salt. Toss together cooled macaroni, cheese, celery, green pepper, and onion. Pour sour cream mixture over all; toss lightly to mix. (Salad will appear quite moist.) Chill several hours or overnight. Makes 12 servings.

Marinated Three-Bean Salad

1 8½-ounce can lima beans,
  drained
1 8-ounce can cut green
  beans, drained
1 8-ounce can red kidney
  beans, drained
1 medium sweet onion, sliced
  and separated into rings
  (½ cup)
½ cup chopped green pepper
⅔ cup vinegar
½ cup salad oil
¼ cup sugar
1 teaspoon celery seed

In large bowl combine the lima beans, green beans, red kidney beans, onion rings, and chopped green pepper. In a screw-top jar combine vinegar, salad oil, sugar, and celery seed; cover and shake to mix well. Pour vinegar mixture over vegetables and stir lightly. Cover and refrigerate several hours or overnight, stirring occasionally. Drain before serving. Makes 8 servings.

Hot Five-Bean Salad

8 slices bacon
⅔ cup sugar
2 tablespoons cornstarch
1½ teaspoons salt
  Dash pepper
¾ cup vinegar
½ cup water
1 16-ounce can dark red
  kidney beans
1 16-ounce can cut green
  beans
1 16-ounce can lima beans
1 16-ounce can cut wax beans
1 15-ounce can garbanzo
  beans

In large skillet cook bacon till crisp; drain, reserving ¼ cup drippings in skillet. Crumble bacon and set aside. Combine sugar, cornstarch, salt, and pepper; blend into reserved drippings. Stir in vinegar and water; cook and stir till boiling. Drain all beans; stir beans into the skillet. Cover and simmer for 15 to 20 minutes. Stir in crumbled bacon. Transfer to a serving dish. Makes 10 to 12 servings.

Creamy Lima Cups

1 10-ounce package frozen
   baby lima beans
¼ cup dairy sour cream
1 tablespoon milk
1 tablespoon vinegar
1 tablespoon salad oil
½ clove garlic, minced
½ teaspoon sugar
¼ teaspoon salt
   Dash paprika
½ cup thinly sliced celery
4 lettuce cups

Cook limas according to package directions; drain well. Cool. Blend together dairy sour cream, milk, vinegar, salad oil, garlic, sugar, salt, and paprika. Combine with beans and celery; cover and chill well. To serve, spoon the mixture into 4 lettuce cups. Sprinkle with additional paprika, if desired. Makes 4 servings.

Carrot-Pineapple Toss

½ cup raisins
1 8¼-ounce can pineapple
   slices, drained
2 cups coarsely shredded
   carrot
½ cup mayonnaise or salad
   dressing
1 teaspoon lemon juice
   (optional)

Place raisins in bowl; cover with boiling *water*. Let stand 5 minutes; drain well. Cut pineapple into small pieces; mix pineapple with shredded carrot and raisins. Cover and chill. Just before serving, blend in mayonnaise. Sprinkle with lemon juice, if desired. Makes 4 servings.

Sauerkraut Salad

1 16-ounce can sauerkraut
¼ cup finely chopped celery
¼ cup chopped onion
¼ cup shredded carrot
¾ cup sugar
¼ cup vinegar

Drain and snip sauerkraut, reserving liquid. Rinse sauerkraut under cold running water. Drain well. Combine sauerkraut, celery, onion, and carrot. In saucepan combine reserved sauerkraut liquid, sugar, and vinegar; bring to boil, stirring constantly. Remove from heat; pour over vegetable mixture. Toss to coat vegetables evenly. Chill several hours or overnight. Makes 6 servings.

Wilted Cabbage Salad

3 slices bacon
¼ cup chopped onion
2 tablespoons vinegar
2 tablespoons water
1 tablespoon sugar
½ teaspoon salt
⅛ teaspoon pepper
1 small head cabbage,
   shredded (about 4 cups)
1 apple, peeled, cored, and
   finely chopped (1 cup)

In skillet cook bacon till crisp; drain, reserving 3 tablespoons drippings. Set bacon aside. Add onion to drippings and cook till tender. Stir in vinegar, water, sugar, salt, and pepper; bring to boiling. Add cabbage and apple; toss to coat. Cover and cook over medium heat about 5 minutes or till cabbage is just wilted. Crumble bacon over top and serve. Makes 6 to 8 servings.

Molded Vegetable Salads

Spanish Vegetable Mold (pictured above)

1 6-ounce package lemon-
   flavored gelatin
1 12-ounce can (1½ cups)
   vegetable juice cocktail
¼ cup Italian salad dressing
3 tablespoons vinegar
1 8-ounce can red kidney beans
½ of a 15-ounce can (¾ cup)
   garbanzo beans
¾ cup tiny cauliflowerets
½ cup chopped, seeded tomato
½ cup chopped celery
⅓ cup chopped green pepper

In bowl dissolve gelatin in 1½ cups boiling *water*. Stir in vegetable juice cocktail, Italian salad dressing, and vinegar. Chill till partially set. Drain the kidney beans and garbanzo beans. Fold beans, cauliflowerets, tomato, celery, and green pepper into gelatin mixture. Turn into a 6½-cup mold. Chill till firm. Unmold onto serving plate. Garnish with curly endive and avocado slices, if desired. Makes 10 to 12 servings.

One Cup Cottage Ring

1 3-ounce package lime-
   flavored gelatin
1 cup mayonnaise *or* salad
   dressing
1 8-ounce carton cream-style
   cottage cheese
1 cup finely chopped celery
1 cup diced green pepper

Dissolve gelatin in 1 cup boiling *water*. Add mayonnaise or salad dressing and beat with rotary beater or electric mixer till smooth. Chill till partially set. Fold in cottage cheese, chopped celery, and diced green pepper. Pour into 4-cup ring mold. Chill till firm. Unmold onto serving plate. Makes 6 servings.

Cucumber Ring Supreme (pictured on page 7)

1 3-ounce package lemon-
   flavored gelatin
1 cup boiling water
¾ cup cold water
3 tablespoons lemon juice
1 cucumber, thinly sliced
2 tablespoons sugar
1 envelope unflavored gelatin
¾ teaspoon salt
¾ cup water
2 tablespoons lemon juice
1 8-ounce package cream
   cheese, cubed and softened
4 cucumbers
1 cup mayonnaise or salad
   dressing
¼ cup snipped parsley
3 tablespoons fincly chopped
   onion

Dissolve lemon-flavored gelatin in boiling water; add the ¾ cup cold water and 3 tablespoons lemon juice. Pour into a deep 6½-cup ring mold. Chill till partially set. Overlap the thinly sliced cucumber atop gelatin mixture in mold; press into gelatin. Chill till almost firm.

Meanwhile, in saucepan mix the sugar, unflavored gelatin, and salt. Add the ¾ cup water; stir over low heat till gelatin and sugar dissolve. Stir in the 2 tablespoons lemon juice. With rotary beater gradually beat hot gelatin mixture into softened cream cheese till mixture is smooth.

Peel and halve the 4 cucumbers lengthwise; scrape out seeds. Grind, using fine blade or finely shred cucumbers. Drain; measure about 1½ cups. Stir ground or shredded cucumber, mayonnaise, parsley, and onion into cream cheese mixture. Pour over almost firm gelatin in mold. Chill till firm. Unmold onto lettuce-lined plate; garnish with cherry tomatoes, if dcsired. Makes 8 to 10 servings.

Perfection Salad

1 6-ounce package lemon-
   flavored gelatin
3¼ cups boiling water
⅓ cup white vinegar
2 tablespoons lemon juice
¾ teaspoon salt
2 cups shredded cabbage
1 cup chopped celery
½ cup chopped green
   pepper (1 medium)
¼ cup sliced pimiento-stuffed
   olives

Dissolve lemon gelatin in boiling water. Stir in vinegar, lemon juice, and salt. Chill mixture till partially set. Fold in cabbage, celery, green pepper, and olives. Turn mixture into a 5½-cup mold. Chill till firm. Unmold salad onto plate. Makes 10 servings.

Broccoli Ring

1 10-ounce package frozen
   chopped broccoli
1 envelope unflavored gelatin
½ cup water
1 10¾-ounce can condensed
   chicken broth
⅔ cup mayonnaise or salad
   dressing
⅓ cup dairy sour cream
1 tablespoon finely chopped
   onion
1 tablespoon lemon juice
3 hard-cooked eggs, chopped

Cook broccoli according to package directions; drain well. Chop broccoli fine. Meanwhile, in medium saucepan soften gelatin in water; add chicken broth. Heat and stir till gelatin is dissolved. Add mayonnaise, sour cream, onion, and lemon juice; beat smooth with rotary beater. Chill till partially set. Fold chopped eggs and broccoli into gelatin. Turn into 4-cup mold. Chill till firm. Unmold onto serving plate. Makes 8 servings.

Like your Italian salad chilled? All the makings for the traditional tossed version go into this refreshing *Italian Salad Mold.*

Creamy Vegetable Mold gets a rich, smooth taste from sour cream sauce mix, a tangy bite from lemon juice, and a delightful herb flavor from dillweed.

Italian Salad Mold (opposite, above)

1 6-ounce package lemon-
  flavored gelatin
½ of a 0.6-ounce envelope (2½
  teaspoons) Italian
  salad dressing mix
1½ cups boiling water
2 cups cold water
¼ cup vinegar
1 cup chopped iceberg
  lettuce
1 cup quartered and thinly
  sliced zucchini
½ cup shredded carrot
¼ cup sliced radishes
  Curly endive

In bowl combine gelatin and salad dressing mix. Add boiling water, stirring to dissolve gelatin. Stir in cold water and vinegar. Chill till partially set. Fold chopped lettuce, zucchini, carrot, and radishes into gelatin. Pour mixture into 5½-cup mold. Chill till firm. To serve, unmold and garnish with curly endive, if desired. Makes 8 servings.

Creamy Vegetable Mold (opposite, below)

2 1.25-ounce packages sour
  cream sauce mix
1 6-ounce package lemon-
  flavored gelatin
2 cups boiling water
½ cup cold water
2 tablespoons lemon juice
¾ teaspoon dried dillweed
2 small carrots, cut up
1 medium green pepper, seeded
  and cut up
1 medium cucumber, peeled,
  seeded, and cut up

Prepare sour cream sauce mixes according to package directions; let stand 10 minutes. Dissolve gelatin in boiling water. Stir in the prepared sour cream sauce, cold water, lemon juice, and dillweed. Beat with rotary beater till blended. Chill till partially set. Put carrots in blender container; cover with cold water. Cover; blend a few seconds or till coarsely chopped. Drain well. Repeat with green pepper and cucumber. Fold chopped vegetables into gelatin mixture. Turn into 5½-cup mold. Chill till firm. To serve, unmold and fill center with assorted fresh vegetables, if desired. Makes 8 servings.

Imperial Garden Salad

⅓ cup sugar
2 envelopes unflavored
  gelatin
1 14-ounce can beef broth
2 cups cold water
2 tablespoons lemon juice
2 tablespoons soy sauce
1 tablespoon vinegar
¼ teaspoon salt
1 16-ounce can fancy mixed
  Chinese vegetables,
  drained
¼ cup diced green pepper
½ cup dairy sour cream
1 tablespoon milk
2 teaspoons soy sauce

In saucepan combine sugar and gelatin. Add beef broth; bring to boiling, stirring to dissolve gelatin. Remove from heat; add cold water, lemon juice, 2 tablespoons soy sauce, vinegar, and salt. Chill till partially set. Fold in Chinese vegetables and green pepper. Pour mixture into 5-cup mold. Chill till firm. To make dressing, combine sour cream, milk, and 2 teaspoons soy sauce. To serve, unmold salad; serve with the dressing. Makes 6 servings.

Garden-Fresh Tomato Aspic

8 large tomatoes
1 3-ounce package lemon-
flavored gelatin
2 tablespoons catsup
1 tablespoon lemon juice
2 teaspoons prepared horseradish
1½ teaspoons worcestershire
sauce
½ teaspoon salt
Dash pepper
¾ cup finely chopped celery
¼ cup finely chopped onion
¼ cup finely chopped green
pepper
Spinach leaves
Mayonnaise *or* salad
dressing

Cut off stems of tomatoes. Prepare tomato shells by scooping out pulp; reserve pulp. To drain, invert tomato shells on paper toweling. Place reserved pulp in blender container. Cover; blend till pureed. Sieve to remove seeds. Measure 2 cups puree. In saucepan combine puree and gelatin. Bring to boiling; stir to dissolve gelatin. Remove from heat; stir in catsup, lemon juice, horseradish, worcestershire, salt, and pepper. Chill till partially set. Fold celery, onion, and green pepper into gelatin mixture. Sprinkle insides of tomato shells with salt; place upright on tray. Fill with gelatin mixture. Chill till firm. Serve on spinach leaves with mayonnaise, if desired. Makes 6 servings.

Tomato Soup Salad

1 10¾-ounce can condensed
tomato soup
1 envelope unflavored
gelatin
¼ teaspoon salt
1 cup cream-style cottage
cheese
¼ cup mayonnaise *or* salad
dressing
1 cup chopped celery
1 cup chopped radishes
½ cup chopped cucumber
2 tablespoons sliced green
onion

In medium saucepan stir together soup, gelatin, and salt; let stand 10 minutes to soften gelatin. Stir over low heat till gelatin dissolves. With rotary beater or electric mixer, beat in cottage cheese and mayonnaise or salad dressing. Chill mixture till partially set. Fold in celery, radishes, cucumber, and green onion. Pour into 4-cup mold. Chill till firm. To serve, unmold onto serving platter. Makes 6 to 8 servings.

Cheesy Coleslaw Mold

1 3-ounce package lime-
flavored gelatin
1½ cups boiling water
2 tablespoons vinegar
⅓ cup mayonnaise *or* salad
dressing
½ teaspoon salt
Dash pepper
1 cup chopped cabbage
½ cup shredded carrot
½ cup shredded sharp
American cheese (2
ounces)
⅛ teaspoon celery seed

Dissolve gelatin in boiling water; stir in vinegar. Add mayonnaise, salt, and pepper; beat smooth with rotary beater. Chill till partially set. Fold cabbage, carrot, cheese, and celery seed into gelatin. Pour into 6 individual molds. Chill till firm. To serve, unmold salads onto lettuce-lined plates, if desired. Makes 6 servings.

Gazpacho Salad

1 envelope unflavored
   gelatin
½ cup cold water
1 10¾-ounce can con-
   densed tomato soup
1 tablespoon white wine
   vinegar
   Several drops bottled
   hot pepper sauce
1 medium tomato, chopped
½ cup peeled, seeded,
   shredded cucumber
½ cup chopped green pepper
¼ cup finely chopped onion
1 6-ounce carton frozen
   avocado dip, thawed
¼ cup mayonnaise or salad
   dressing
¼ cup dairy sour cream
1 tablespoon lemon juice
   Several drops bottled
   hot pepper sauce

In small saucepan soften gelatin in cold water. Stir in soup, vinegar, and several drops of hot pepper sauce; stir till gelatin dissolves. Chill mixture till partially set. Fold tomato, cucumber, green pepper, and onion into gelatin mixture. Pour into a 3-cup mold. Chill till firm. To make dressing, combine avocado dip, mayonnaise or salad dressing, sour cream, lemon juice, and several drops hot pepper sauce. To serve, unmold salad and serve with the dressing. Makes 4 or 5 servings.

Cottage Cheese-Cucumber Salad

1 3-ounce package lemon-
   flavored gelatin
1 cup boiling water
2 tablespoons lemon juice
1 teaspoon grated onion
1 cup cream-style cottage
   cheese, drained
1 cup very finely chopped
   cucumber

Dissolve gelatin in boiling water. Add lemon juice and onion. Chill till partially set. Beat till light and fluffy. Fold cheese and cucumber into gelatin mixture. Pour into 6 individual molds; chill till firm. To serve, unmold on lettuce-lined plates, if desired. Makes 6 servings.

Barbecue Bean Mold

2 envelopes unflavored
   gelatin
½ cup tomato juice
1 tablespoon brown sugar
1 teaspoon prepared mustard
1 cup tomato juice
2 tablespoons lemon juice
1 15¾-ounce can barbecue
   beans
½ cup chopped celery
1 tablespoon finely chopped
   onion

In saucepan soften gelatin in the ½ cup tomato juice. Add brown sugar and prepared mustard; stir over low heat till gelatin and sugar dissolve. Stir in the 1 cup tomato juice and the lemon juice. Chill till partially set.

Fold barbecue beans, celery, and onion into gelatin mixture. Pour into 4-cup mold. Chill till firm. Unmold onto serving plate. Makes 6 servings.

2 FRESH FRUIT SALADS

The pert, sweet flavor of fresh fruit opens an entire world of delicious salad creations. Favorite fruit combinations come together in spectacular fresh fruit platters, impressive layered compotes, glistening gelatin molds, and icy fruit mixtures from the freezer. Here are some of our fresh-picked favorites: *Strawberry-Melon Salad* (front, left), *Tossed Fruit Salad* (back, center), *Grape and Grapefruit Mold* (front, right), and *Pineapple-Berry Boat* (back, right). (See index for recipe pages.)

Fabulous Fruit Bowls

Tossed Fruit Salad (pictured on page 38)

½ cup sugar
¼ cup tarragon vinegar
2 tablespoons water
1 teaspoon celery salt
1 teaspoon paprika
1 teaspoon dry mustard
1 cup salad oil
2 medium oranges, chilled
1 medium grapefruit,
  chilled
1 ripe medium banana
4 cups torn iceberg lettuce
2 cups torn escarole
1 avocado, peeled and thinly
  sliced
1 cup red grapes, halved
  and seeded

To make dressing, in saucepan combine sugar, vinegar, and water. Heat and stir just till sugar dissolves; cool. Stir in celery salt, paprika, and mustard. Add oil in slow stream, beating with electric mixer till thick. Cover and chill.

Peel and section oranges and grapefruit, reserving juices. Peel and slice banana; brush with reserved citrus juices. Set aside. In large salad bowl combine iceberg lettuce and escarole. Arrange orange and grapefruit sections, banana, avocado slices, and grapes in a circle atop lettuce. Pour on chilled dressing. Toss to coat fruit and vegetables. Makes 6 to 8 servings.

Fruit Salad Platter (opposite)

1 pineapple
1 pint strawberries
1 papaya
¼ cup orange juice
2 cups honeydew melon balls
1 cantaloupe, peeled, seeded, and sliced
Lettuce
Honey-Lime Dressing
Spicy Nectar Dressing
Strawberry-Cheese Dressing

Rinse pineapple. Twist off the crown and cut off the base. Slice off strips of rind lengthwise, then cut out and discard eyes. Slice the fruit in spears; cut off hard core. Cover spears; chill. Rinse strawberries; drain and chill. Peel and slice papaya; dip in orange juice. Chill. Thoroughly chill honeydew balls and cantaloupe.

On large lettuce-lined platter arrange fruit. Serve with *Honey-Lime Dressing*, *Spicy Nectar Dressing*, and *Strawberry-Cheese Dressing*. Makes 8 servings.

Honey-Lime Dressing: In small mixer bowl blend together ½ cup *honey*, ¼ teaspoon finely shredded *lime peel*, ¼ cup *lime juice*, ¼ teaspoon *salt*, and ¼ teaspoon ground *mace*. Gradually add ¾ cup *salad oil*, beating with electric mixer or rotary beater till mixture is thickened. Beat in 2 drops green food coloring. Cover; chill. Makes 1½ cups.

Spicy Nectar Dressing: In small mixer bowl combine 1 cup dairy *sour cream*, ½ cup *apricot nectar*, ½ cup *salad oil*, 3 tablespoons *sugar*, ½ teaspoon ground *cinnamon*, ½ teaspoon *paprika*, and dash *salt*. Beat ingredients together with electric mixer or rotary beater till mixture is smooth. Cover dressing and chill thoroughly. Makes 1¾ cups.

Strawberry-Cheese Dressing: In small mixer bowl beat together one 3-ounce package *cream cheese*, softened; ½ of a 10-ounce package (½ cup) frozen *strawberries*, thawed; 1 tablespoon *sugar;* 1 tablespoon *lemon juice;* and dash *salt*. Gradually add ½ cup *salad oil*, beating till mixture is thickened. Beat in 1 or 2 drops *red food coloring*. Cover and chill thoroughly. Makes 1⅓ cups.

Pineapple-Berry Boat (pictured on page 39)

2 medium pineapples
2 pints raspberries *or* strawberries
⅓ cup raspberry preserves
1 3-ounce package cream cheese, softened
1 tablespoon milk
½ teaspoon finely shredded lemon peel
2 teaspoons lemon juice
½ cup whipping cream

Halve pineapples lengthwise. Using a sharp knife, cut out the pineapple meat, leaving shell intact. Cut off the hard core and cut pineapple into chunks. Combine pineapple chunks and raspberries or strawberries; mound into pineapple shells. To make dressing, gradually blend the preserves into softened cream cheese. Stir in the milk, lemon peel, and lemon juice. Whip cream just till soft peaks form; fold into cream cheese mixture. Chill. Spoon dressing over pineapple-filled shells. Serve fruit salad from shells. Makes 8 servings.

Strawberry-Melon Salad (pictured on page 38)

2 small honeydew melons
Leaf lettuce
1½ cups cream-style cottage cheese
1 cup strawberries

Cut melons in half and remove seeds. Use a melon baller to scoop out pulp. Line melon shells with leaf lettuce. Divide melon balls among lined shells. Mound a generous ⅓ cup cottage cheese in center of each. Place ¼ cup strawberries around each mound. Makes 4 servings.

Waldorf Salad is one of the easiest fruit salads to prepare, and one of the most popular. Just combine apples, celery, grapes, and walnuts, then stir in the creamy dressing.

When it comes to a tasty fruit combination, you can't top *Rainbow Compote.* Fresh strawberries, honeydew melon cubes, blueberries, and orange slices team well with a candied ginger-fruit syrup.

Waldorf Salad (opposite, above)

4 medium apples, cored and
   chopped (3 cups)
½ cup chopped celery
½ cup red grapes, halved and
   seeded
½ cup chopped walnuts
   Romaine
½ cup mayonnaise *or* salad
   dressing
1 tablespoon sugar
½ teaspoon lemon juice
½ cup whipping cream
   Ground nutmeg

Combine apples, celery, grapes, and walnuts. Turn fruit mixture into a romaine-lined salad bowl; chill. Combine mayonnaise or salad dressing, sugar, and lemon juice. Whip cream till soft peaks form; fold into mayonnaise mixture. Spoon the dressing over the chilled apple mixture. Sprinkle lightly with nutmeg. To serve, fold dressing into fruit mixture. Makes 6 servings.

Rainbow Compote (opposite, below)

½ cup honey
2 tablespoons lemon juice
1 tablespoon finely snipped
   candied ginger (optional)
1 teaspoon finely shredded
   orange peel
4 oranges, peeled and sliced
   crosswise
1½ cups blueberries
2 cups cubed honeydew melon
1½ cups halved strawberries
   Whole strawberries

Combine honey, lemon juice, candied ginger, and orange peel. Pour dressing over orange slices in bowl; cover and refrigerate for several hours or overnight. Chill the remaining fruits. Drain oranges, reserving dressing. Arrange orange slices in bottom of compote. Top with a layer of blueberries, a layer of melon cubes, and a layer of halved strawberries. Pour the reserved dressing over fruit. Garnish with additional whole strawberries, if desired. Makes 10 servings.

Tropical Fruit Salad

¼ cup mayonnaise *or* salad
   dressing
1 tablespoon sugar
½ teaspoon lemon juice
   Dash salt
½ cup whipping cream
1 large red apple,
   chopped (1 cup)
1 large yellow delicious
   apple, chopped (1 cup)
1 large banana, sliced
1 cup sliced celery
½ cup broken walnuts
   Lettuce
½ cup toasted flaked coconut
   Unpeeled apple slices

Blend together mayonnaise or salad dressing, sugar, lemon juice, and salt. Whip the cream till soft peaks form; fold into the mayonnaise mixture. Gently fold in the red and yellow apple, banana, celery, and walnuts. Chill.

Line salad bowl with lettuce; spoon in the chilled fruit mixture. Garnish with toasted coconut. Top with additional apple slices, if desired. Makes 6 servings.

24-Hour Fruit Salad

1 20-ounce can pineapple
  chunks
3 slightly beaten egg yolks
2 tablespoons sugar
2 tablespoons vinegar
1 tablespoon butter *or*
  margarine
  Dash salt
1 17-ounce can pitted light
  sweet cherries, drained
3 oranges, peeled, sectioned,
  and drained
2 cups tiny marshmallows
1 cup whipping cream

Drain pineapple; reserve 2 tablespoons syrup. To make custard, in small heavy saucepan combine reserved syrup, egg yolks, sugar, vinegar, butter or margarine, and salt. Cook and stir over low heat about 6 minutes or till mixture thickens slightly and coats a metal spoon. Cool to room temperature. In large bowl combine pineapple, cherries, oranges, and marshmallows. Pour custard over; mix fruit mixture gently. Whip the whipping cream till soft peaks form. Fold whipped cream into fruit mixture. Turn into serving bowl. Cover and refrigerate 24 hours or overnight. Makes 10 to 12 servings.

5-Cup Salad

1 11-ounce can mandarin
  orange sections, drained
1 8¼-ounce can pineapple
  chunks, drained
1 cup flaked *or* shredded
  coconut
1 cup tiny marshmallows
1 cup dairy sour cream

In bowl combine mandarin orange sections, pineapple chunks, coconut, marshmallows, and sour cream. Cover and refrigerate for several hours or overnight. Makes 6 to 8 servings.

Orange-Cream Fruit Salad

1 20-ounce can pineapple
  chunks, drained
1 16-ounce can peach slices,
  drained
1 11-ounce can mandarin orange
  sections, drained
3 medium bananas, sliced
2 medium apples, cored and
  chopped
1 3½- *or* 3¾-ounce
  package *instant* vanilla
  pudding mix
1½ cups milk
½ of a 6-ounce can (⅓ cup)
  frozen orange juice concentrate, thawed
¾ cup dairy sour cream
  Lettuce cups

In large bowl combine pineapple chunks, peaches, orange sections, bananas, and apples; set aside. In small bowl combine dry pudding mix, milk, and orange juice concentrate. Beat with rotary beater 1 to 2 minutes or till well blended. Beat in sour cream. Fold into the fruit mixture. Cover and refrigerate several hours.

Serve the salad in lettuce cups on individual serving plates. Makes 10 servings.

Cinnamon-Apple Salads

½ cup red cinnamon candies
2 cups water
6 small tart apples, peeled
   and cored
1 3-ounce package cream cheese,
   softened
2 tablespoons milk
1 teaspoon lemon juice
1 8¼-ounce can crushed
   pineapple, drained
⅓ cup snipped pitted dates
2 tablespoons chopped
   walnuts
   Lettuce

In 3-quart saucepan cook and stir cinnamon candies in water till dissolved. Add apples and cook slowly, uncovered, for 15 to 20 minutes or just till tender, turning once during cooking. Chill apples in syrup several hours, turning once. Blend together cream cheese, milk, and lemon juice till smooth. Stir in pineapple, dates, and walnuts. Drain apples; stuff center of each apple with some of the cream cheese mixture. Serve on lettuce-lined plates. Makes 6 servings.

Ambrosia Salad

1 15¼-ounce can pineapple
   chunks
3 medium oranges, peeled
   and sectioned
½ cup maraschino
   cherries, halved and
   drained
½ cup flaked *or* shredded
   coconut
   Fresh mint leaves

Drain pineapple chunks, reserving ¼ cup of the syrup. Combine pineapple chunks, the ¼ cup reserved pineapple syrup, orange sections, and maraschino cherries. Cover; chill thoroughly. Just before serving, fold in coconut. Garnish with fresh mint leaves, if desired. Makes 6 servings.

Sunshine Salad

½ of 21-ounce can (1 cup)
   apricot pie filling
½ of 14-ounce can (⅔ cup)
   sweetened condensed
   milk
½ of 4½-ounce carton frozen
   whipped dessert topping,
   thawed
¼ cup lemon juice
2 11-ounce cans mandarin
   orange sections, drained
1 15¼-ounce can pineapple
   chunks, drained
½ cup tiny marshmallows
½ cup chopped walnuts
¼ cup flaked *or* shredded
   coconut

In large bowl combine pie filling, condensed milk, whipped topping, and lemon juice. Reserve several mandarin orange sections. Fold remaining mandarin oranges into apricot mixture along with pineapple, marshmallows, chopped walnuts, and coconut. Cover and refrigerate several hours or overnight. Garnish salad with reserved oranges and sprinkle with additional coconut, if desired. Makes 8 to 10 servings.

Molded Fruit Salads

Harvest Fruit Mold (pictured above)

1 12-ounce package mixed dried
   fruits
¼ cup sugar
1 6-ounce package orange-
   flavored gelatin
2 cups boiling water
½ cup dry sherry
   Leaf lettuce
   Frosted Grapes
   Preserved kumquats, halved
   lengthwise

In saucepan combine dried fruit and enough water to cover the fruit. Simmer gently, covered, for 25 minutes. Add sugar; simmer 5 to 10 minutes more. Drain fruit, reserving syrup. Add water to syrup to make 1½ cups liquid. Dissolve gelatin in boiling water. Stir in reserved syrup mixture and sherry. Chill till partially set.

Pit prunes; cut up all cooked fruit. Fold into gelatin mixture. Pour into 6-cup ring mold. Chill till firm. Unmold on lettuce-lined platter. Fill center of mold with *Frosted Grapes*. Garnish with kumquat halves. Serves 8 to 10.

Frosted Grapes: Dip 1½ pounds *green grapes* into 2 lightly beaten *egg whites.* Drain. Dip grapes in ½ cup *sugar.* Place on rack to dry for 2 hours.

Grape and Grapefruit Mold (pictured on page 39)

2 envelopes unflavored gelatin
½ cup sugar
1 cup boiling water
1 16-ounce can sweetened
   grapefruit sections
   Unsweetened grapefruit juice
   (about 1¼ cups)
¼ cup lemon juice
   Several drops yellow food
   coloring
2 cups seedless green grapes
   Lettuce

Dissolve gelatin and sugar in boiling water. Drain grapefruit, reserving syrup. Add enough unsweetened grapefruit juice to reserved syrup to make 2¼ cups. Add to gelatin mixture with lemon juice and food coloring. Chill till partially set. Fold grapefruit and grapes into gelatin. Carefully pour into 6-cup mold. Or, arrange a few of the grapes in bottom of mold; add gelatin to cover. Chill till almost set. Repeat with remaining grapes, the grapefruit, and gelatin, arranging fruit along sides of mold. Chill till firm. Unmold on lettuce-lined platter. Makes 10 to 12 servings.

Jubilee Salad Mold

1 10-ounce package frozen
   red raspberries, thawed
1 6-ounce package red raspberry-flavored gelatin
1¾ cups boiling water
½ cup cream sherry
¼ cup lemon juice
1 16-ounce can pitted dark
   sweet cherries, drained
   and halved

Drain raspberries, reserving syrup. In large mixing bowl dissolve gelatin in boiling water. Stir in sherry, lemon juice, and reserved raspberry syrup. Chill till partially set. Fold in raspberries and cherries. Pour into a 5- or 6-cup ring mold. Chill till firm. Unmold on lettuce-lined platter, if desired. Makes 8 servings.

Fruity Ginger Ale Mold (pictured on cover)

1 3-ounce package lemon-
   flavored gelatin
1 cup boiling water
1 cup ginger ale, chilled
1 medium apple, cored and
   cut in wedges
1 8¼-ounce can pineapple
   slices, cut up
1 small apple, cored, peeled,
   and chopped
½ cup halved seedless green
   grapes

Dissolve gelatin in boiling water. Cool to room temperature. Slowly add ginger ale.

Arrange apple wedges in 4½-cup mold. Pour in ¾ cup of the gelatin mixture. Chill till almost firm. Meanwhile, chill remaining gelatin till partially set. Fold in pineapple, chopped apple, and halved grapes. Pour over first layer. Chill till firm. Unmold on lettuce-lined platter, if desired. Makes 5 or 6 servings.

Unmolding a Gelatin Salad

Tower or ring gelatin salads aren't tricky to unmold if you follow these steps and helpful hints. With the tip of a small paring knife, loosen edge of gelatin from the mold (and around center of ring mold). (A) Dip the mold just to the rim in warm water for a *few seconds*. Tilt slightly to ease gelatin away from one side and let air in. Tilt and rotate mold so air can loosen gelatin all the way around. (B) Center an upside-down serving plate over the mold. Holding tightly, invert plate and mold. Shake mold gently. (C) Lift off the mold, being careful not to tear the gelatin. If the salad doesn't slide out easily, repeat the process, beginning with step A. Garnish serving plate, if desired.

Pear-Limeade Molds (opposite, above)

2 envelopes unflavored gelatin
½ cup cold water
2 pears, peeled, halved, and
    cored
2 cups water
¼ cup sugar
1 6-ounce can frozen limeade
    concentrate
    Dash salt
    Green food coloring
    Whole maraschino cherries
    Endive
    Mayonnaise *or* salad
    dressing
    Chopped pecans

Soften gelatin in cold water; set aside. In saucepan combine pear halves, the 2 cups water, and the sugar. Bring mixture to boil; reduce heat. Cover and simmer 5 to 6 minutes or till pears are tender. With slotted spoon, remove pears to a bowl; cover and refrigerate. Stir softened gelatin into hot pear liquid, stirring till dissolved. Add limeade concentrate, salt, and a few drops of food coloring. Pour *⅓ cup* of the gelatin mixture into each of 4 flared water goblets or tall individual molds. Chill till almost firm. Chill the remaining gelatin till partially set. Add a pear half, narrow end down, to each goblet, tucking a maraschino cherry into each. Cover the pears with remaining gelatin. Chill till firm. Unmold on plates, flared end down. Garnish with endive. Spoon some mayonnaise or salad dressing atop and sprinkle with chopped pecans, if desired. Makes 4 servings.

Lemon-Frosted Plum Squares (opposite, below left)

1 6-ounce package strawberry-
    flavored gelatin
    Dash salt
2½ cups boiling water
1 cup lemon-lime
    carbonated beverage
2 tablespoons lemon juice
2 cups plums, pitted and cut in
    wedges (9 plums)
1 3½- *or* 3¾-ounce package
    instant lemon pudding mix
1¼ cups cold milk
½ cup dairy sour cream
    Bibb lettuce
    Apple slices

Dissolve gelatin and salt in boiling water. Cool to room temperature. Slowly pour in carbonated beverage and lemon juice; stir gently. Chill till partially set. Fold in plums. Pour into 8×8×2-inch pan. Chill till almost firm. In mixer bowl combine pudding mix and milk; beat till smooth. Blend in sour cream. Spread pudding mixture atop gelatin. Chill till firm. Cut into squares and serve on lettuce-lined plates. Garnish with apple slices atop each square, if desired. Makes 6 to 8 servings.

Apricot Soufflé Salad (opposite, below right)

1 3-ounce package orange-
    flavored gelatin
1 cup boiling water
½ cup cold water
2 tablespoons lemon juice
⅓ cup mayonnaise *or* salad
    dressing
2 tablespoons finely chopped
    celery
4 *or* 5 apricots, peeled
    and sliced (1 cup)
1 medium apple, thinly sliced

Dissolve gelatin in boiling water. Stir in cold water and lemon juice. Chill till partially set; whip till fluffy. On low speed of mixer, beat in mayonnaise or salad dressing. Fold in celery. Arrange apricot and apple slices in a 5 to 5½ cup mold; carefully spoon in gelatin. Chill till firm. Makes 4 to 6 servings.

Tall, shimmering, and definitely fancy describe *Pear-Limeade Molds.* To make this graceful tower salad, use a stemmed water goblet to mold the pear half and gelatin.

For a fast make-ahead salad, fix *Lemon-Frosted Plum Squares.*

Treat your guests to the rich flavor of *Apricot Soufflé Salad.*

Cherry-Cider Salad (opposite, above)

2 cups apple cider *or* apple
   juice
1 6-ounce package cherry-
   flavored gelatin
1 16-ounce can pitted dark
   sweet cherries
½ cup thinly sliced celery
½ cup chopped walnuts
1 3-ounce package cream
   cheese, softened
1 8½-ounce can (1 cup)
   applesauce
   Leaf lettuce

Bring apple cider or juice to boiling. Dissolve gelatin in boiling cider. Drain cherries, reserving syrup. Halve cherries and set aside. Add enough water to reserved syrup to measure 1½ cups liquid; stir into gelatin. Set aside 2 cups of the gelatin mixture; keep at room temperature. Chill remaining gelatin till partially set. Fold cherries, celery, and walnuts into partially set gelatin. Pour into 6½-cup ring mold. Chill till almost firm. Gradually add reserved gelatin to softened cream cheese, beating till smooth. Stir in applesauce. Spoon cream cheese mixture over cherry layer in mold. Chill till firm. Unmold on lettuce-lined platter. Serve with mayonnaise or salad dressing and sprinkle with additional walnuts, if desired. Makes 10 to 12 servings.

Strawberry Soufflé Salads (opposite, below)

1 10-ounce package frozen
   sliced strawberries,
   thawed
1 3-ounce package strawberry-
   flavored gelatin
1 cup boiling water
2 tablespoons lemon juice
¼ cup mayonnaise *or*
   salad dressing
¼ cup chopped walnuts
   Romaine
   Canned pineapple slices

Drain strawberries, reserving syrup. Add enough water to syrup to make ¾ cup liquid. Dissolve gelatin and ¼ teaspoon *salt* in boiling water. Stir in reserved syrup and lemon juice. Beat in mayonnaise or salad dressing. Chill till partially set. With electric mixer whip gelatin mixture till fluffy. Fold in strawberries and nuts. Pour into 4 to 6 individual molds. Chill till firm. Unmold onto a lettuce-lined platter, setting each salad atop a pineapple slice. Serve with additional mayonnaise or salad dressing, if desired. Makes 4 to 6 servings.

Minted Pear Salad

1 14-ounce can *or* jar mint-
   flavored pear halves
1 3-ounce package lime-
   flavored gelatin
1 cup boiling water
1 8-ounce carton plain yogurt

Drain pears, reserving ½ cup of the syrup. Dissolve gelatin in boiling water; stir in reserved pear syrup. Chill till partially set. Beat into yogurt. Chop pear halves; fold into gelatin. Pour into 9×5×3-inch loaf pan. Chill till firm. Cut in rectangles to serve. Makes 6 servings.

Gooseberry-Banana Salad

1 16-ounce can gooseberries
1 3-ounce package lime-
   flavored gelatin
1 3-ounce package lemon-
   flavored gelatin
1 pint lime sherbet
2 bananas, sliced
½ cup thinly sliced celery

Drain gooseberries, reserving syrup; add enough water to syrup to make 2 cups liquid. Heat gooseberry liquid to boiling. Add lime- and lemon-flavored gelatin, stirring till dissolved. Stir in lime sherbet by tablespoonfuls. Chill till partially set. Stir gooseberries, bananas, and celery into gelatin mixture. Turn into 9×9×2-inch pan. Chill till firm. Cut in squares. Makes 12 servings.

This two-layered gelatin salad is a natural favorite for your fall menu. *Cherry-Cider Salad* offers a flavorful combination of sweet cherries, apple cider, cream cheese, and applesauce.

Individually molded *Strawberry Soufflé Salads* begin with frozen strawberries and strawberry-flavored gelatin. Pineapple slices form the base for these serving-size salads, and lemon juice adds a pleasant, flavorful accent.

Lemon-Papaya Salad

1 3-ounce package lemon-
  flavored gelatin
1 cup boiling water
1 3-ounce package cream cheese,
  softened
1 egg yolk
⅛ teaspoon salt
½ cup dairy sour cream
¼ teaspoon finely shredded
  lemon peel
1½ teaspoons lemon juice
1 stiffly beaten egg white
1 medium papaya, seeded,
  peeled, and diced
  Leaf lettuce

Dissolve gelatin in boiling water; cool to room temperature. In a large mixing bowl combine cream cheese, egg yolk, and salt; mix thoroughly. Stir in sour cream, lemon peel, and lemon juice. Stir cooled gelatin mixture into sour cream mixture. Chill till partially set. Gently fold in egg white and papaya. Chill till amost firm. Turn into a 4-cup ring mold. Chill till firm. Unmold salad on lettuce-lined platter. Makes 6 servings.

Cherry-Orange Squares

3 large oranges
1 6-ounce package cherry-
  flavored gelatin
1 cup boiling water
1 21-ounce can cherry pie
  filling
1 3-ounce package lemon-
  flavored gelatin
1 cup boiling water
½ cup cold water
1 8-ounce carton lemon yogurt
½ cup chopped toasted almonds

Section oranges over a bowl to catch juice; add enough water to juice to make ½ cup liquid. Dice oranges. Dissolve cherry-flavored gelatin in 1 cup boiling water; stir in orange juice. Chill till partially set. Fold in cherry pie filling and oranges. Pour into 12×7×2-inch dish. Chill till almost firm. Meanwhile, dissolve lemon-flavored gelatin in 1 cup boiling water; stir in cold water. Beat in yogurt. Spoon over the cherry layer. Sprinkle with toasted almonds. Chill till firm. Cut in squares to serve. Makes 10 to 12 servings.

Cran-Raspberry Ring

1 3-ounce package
  raspberry-flavored
  gelatin
1 3-ounce package lemon-
  flavored gelatin
1¼ cups boiling water
1 10-ounce package frozen
  red raspberries
1 14-ounce jar cranberry-
  orange relish
1 cup lemon-lime carbonated
  beverage
  Lettuce

Dissolve raspberry- and lemon-flavored gelatin in boiling water. Stir in frozen raspberries, breaking up large pieces with fork. Stir in cranberry-orange relish.

Slowly pour in lemon-lime carbonated beverage; stir gently. Turn into a 6- or 6½-cup ring mold. Chill till firm. Unmold on lettuce-lined platter. Makes 8 to 10 servings.

Cider Waldorf Mold

2 cups apple cider *or* apple juice
1 3-ounce package lemon-flavored gelatin
1 cup finely chopped apple
¼ cup finely chopped celery
¼ cup finely chopped pecans
Lettuce
Mayonnaise *or* salad dressing

Bring *1 cup* apple cider or juice to boiling. Dissolve gelatin in boiling cider. Stir in remaining cider or juice. Chill till partially set. Fold in apple, celery, and pecans. Pour into a 3-cup mold or spoon into 6 individual molds. Chill till firm. Unmold on lettuce-lined plates. Serve with mayonnaise or salad dressing. Makes 6 servings.

Spicy Orange-Fig Mold

1 cup water
2 inches stick cinnamon
10 whole cloves
1 3-ounce package orange-flavored gelatin
1 cup orange juice
1 large apple, peeled, cored, and diced (1 cup)
½ cup chopped dried figs
Lettuce

In small saucepan combine water, stick cinnamon, and cloves; cover and simmer 5 minutes. Remove cinnamon and cloves. Measure liquid; add more boiling water, if necessary, to measure 1 cup. Add gelatin, stirring till dissolved. Stir in orange juice. Chill till partially set. Fold in apple and figs. Pour into 3½-cup mold. Chill till firm. Unmold on lettuce-lined platter. Makes 4 or 5 servings.

Note: If desired, soften dried figs before using. Place figs in strainer; pour boiling water over fruit. Drain well.

Terms to Know about Gelatin

Recipes for gelatin salads frequently refer to different "jellying" stages. Each step in preparing the salad (blending, folding, beating, and layering) should be done while the gelatin is the proper consistency or thickness. Because the consistency of gelatin changes as it chills, it's important to recognize each stage as it occurs. We've listed the terms used to describe the different stages, plus some helpful hints on how to recognize them.

Chill till partially set: The gelatin is the consistency of unbeaten egg whites. At this stage ingredients such as fruit and nuts are folded in. The solid ingredients will neither sink nor float, but remain evenly distributed. If whipped at this stage, the mixture will become fluffy and will mound.

Chill till almost firm: The gelatin mixture appears set, but will tend to flow if tipped to one side and is sticky to the touch. The mixture mounds when dropped from a spoon. This is the desired consistency when preparing a layered salad.

Chill till firm: The gelatin mixture can now hold a distinctive cut and doesn't move when tilted in the mold. The gelatin is completely set and ready to unmold.

54

Frozen Salad Favorites

Frozen Lime-Mint Salads (pictured above)

1 29½-ounce can crushed
   pineapple
1 3-ounce package lime-
   flavored gelatin
1 6½-ounce package tiny
   marshmallows
1 cup butter mints, crushed
1 9-ounce container frozen
   whipped dessert topping,
   thawed
   Grape leaves *or* lettuce

In large bowl combine *undrained* pineapple, *dry* lime gelatin, marshmallows, and crushed mints. Cover and refrigerate for several hours or till marshmallows soften and melt. Fold in dessert topping. Spoon mixture into 16 paper bake-cup-lined muffin pans. Cover and freeze till firm. Peel off paper and serve on grape leaf or lettuce-lined plates. Garnish with fresh mint sprigs, if desired. Makes 16.

Orange-Apricot Freeze

2 8-ounce cartons orange
   yogurt
½ cup sugar
1 17-ounce can unpeeled
   apricot halves, drained
⅓ cup coarsely chopped pecans
   Lettuce

In mixing bowl stir together yogurt and sugar till blended. Cut up apricots. Fold apricots and nuts into yogurt mixture. Spoon into 8 to 10 paper bake-cup-lined muffin pans. Cover and freeze till firm. Peel off paper from salads. Serve on lettuce-lined plates. Makes 8 to 10 servings.

Fruited Avocado Freeze

1 large avocado
2 tablespoons lemon juice
¼ cup mayonnaise *or* salad
  dressing
1 3-ounce package cream
  cheese, softened
2 tablespoons sugar
¼ teaspoon salt
1 16-ounce can pear halves,
  drained and chopped
¼ cup chopped maraschino
  cherries
½ cup whipping cream
  Lettuce

Halve, seed, peel, and chop avocado; sprinkle with *1 table-spoon* of the lemon juice. Blend together the remaining lemon juice, mayonnaise or salad dressing, cream cheese, sugar, and salt. Add chopped avocado, pears, and chopped maraschino cherries. Whip the cream till soft peaks form. Fold into cream cheese mixture. Pour mixture into 7½×3½×2-inch junior loaf pan. Cover and freeze till firm.

To serve, let stand at room temperature about 10 minutes. Unmold. Slice and serve atop lettuce-lined salad plates. Makes 6 to 8 servings.

Frozen Orange-Date Molds

1 8-ounce package cream
  cheese, softened
¼ cup orange juice
1 8¼-ounce can crushed pineapple, drained
½ cup finely snipped pitted
  dates
½ cup chopped pecans
¼ cup maraschino cherries,
  halved
½ teaspoon finely shredded
  orange peel
1 cup whipping cream
  Lettuce

Beat together cream cheese and orange juice till fluffy. Stir in drained pineapple, dates, nuts, cherries, and orange peel. Whip the cream till soft peaks form. Fold whipped cream into cream cheese mixture. Spoon into 9 individual molds or one 8×4×2-inch loaf dish. Cover and freeze till firm. Let stand at room temperature 10 to 15 minutes before serving. Unmold onto lettuce-lined plates. Garnish with orange slices, if desired. Makes 9 servings.

Frozen Lemon Salad

1 8-ounce package cream
  cheese, softened
¼ cup mayonnaise *or* salad
  dressing
1 pint lemon sherbet
1 11-ounce can mandarin
  orange sections, drained
  and cut up
1 8-ounce can peach slices,
  drained and chopped
¼ cup slivered almonds,
  toasted
  Lettuce

In large bowl beat together cream cheese and mayonnaise or salad dressing till smooth. Stir sherbet to soften; quickly stir into cream cheese mixture. Stir in orange sections, peaches, and almonds. Turn cream cheese-fruit mixture into 8×8×2-inch dish. Cover and freeze till firm.

To serve, let stand at room temperature for 10 to 15 minutes. Cut into squares. Serve on lettuce-lined salad plates. Makes 9 to 12 servings.

Frozen Cheesecake Salads

1 10¾- *or* 11-ounce package cheesecake mix
1 8¼-ounce can crushed pineapple
1 cup milk
1 cup cranberries, chopped
½ cup chopped walnuts
½ cup snipped pitted dates

Set aside graham cracker crumb portion of cheesecake mix for another use. (For example, follow package directions to make a graham cracker crust.) In small mixing bowl blend together dry cheesecake mix, *undrained* pineapple, and milk. Beat till slightly thickened. Fold in chopped cranberries, nuts, and dates. Spoon the mixture into 8 to 10 paper bake-cup-lined muffin pans. Cover and freeze till firm. Peel off paper and serve. Makes 8 to 10 servings.

Frozen Strawberry-Banana Salads

1 21-ounce can strawberry pie
   filling
1 pint vanilla ice cream,
   softened
1 tablespoon lemon juice
3 medium bananas, chopped
¼ cup coarsely chopped toasted
   almonds
   Lettuce

Stir together pie filling, softened ice cream, and lemon juice. Stir in bananas and nuts. Turn mixture into 8 individual molds. Cover and freeze till firm. To serve, let stand at room temperature 10 minutes. Unmold onto lettuce-lined plates. Makes 8 servings.

Frozen Fruitcake Salad

1 cup dairy sour cream
½ cup sugar
½ of 4½-ounce container frozen
   whipped dessert topping,
   thawed
2 tablespoons lemon juice
1 teaspoon vanilla
½ cup red candied cherries
½ cup green candied cherries
1 13¼-ounce can crushed
   pineapple, drained
2 medium bananas, chopped
½ cup chopped walnuts
   Lettuce

In mixing bowl blend together sour cream, sugar, dessert topping, lemon juice, and vanilla. Slice the red and green candied cherries. Fold cherries, the drained pineapple, bananas, and nuts into sour cream mixture. Turn mixture into a 4½-cup ring mold. Cover and freeze till firm.

   To serve, let stand at room temperature 10 minutes. Unmold onto lettuce-lined plate. Garnish with additional candied cherries, if desired. Slice to serve. Makes 8 servings.

Frozen Cherry Salad

1 4½-ounce container frozen
   whipped dessert topping,
   thawed
1 4-ounce container whipped
   cream cheese, softened
1 21-ounce can cherry pie
   filling
2 11-ounce cans mandarin
   orange sections, drained

Stir together whipped dessert topping and cream cheese. Fold in pie filling. Set aside 2 or 3 orange sections for garnish; fold remaining oranges into cherry mixture. Line bottom of a 9×5×3-inch loaf pan with waxed paper; pour in cherry mixture. Cover; freeze till firm. To serve, let stand at room temperature 10 minutes. Unmold onto serving platter; discard waxed paper. Garnish with reserved oranges. Slice to serve. Makes 8 to 10 servings.

Frosty Fruit Cubes

1 3½- or 3¾-ounce package
instant vanilla pudding
mix
1 4½-ounce container frozen
whipped dessert topping,
thawed
¼ cup mayonnaise *or* salad
dressing
2 tablespoons lemon juice
2 8¼-ounce cans crushed
pineapple, drained
2 large bananas, chopped
½ cup toasted slivered
almonds
Lettuce

Prepare instant pudding mix according to package directions. Stir in dessert topping, mayonnaise *or* salad dressing, and lemon juice. Combine pineapple, bananas, and almonds. Fold into pudding mixture. Turn mixture into 11×7×1½-inch pan. Cover and freeze till firm.

To serve, let stand at room temperature 10 minutes. Cut into 1-inch cubes; serve on lettuce-lined salad plates. If desired, top with additional toasted almonds. Makes 12 servings.

Frosty Pear Squares

1 4-ounce container whipped
cream cheese
½ cup dairy sour cream
½ of a 6-ounce can (⅓ cup)
frozen limeade concentrate,
thawed
2 tablespoons sugar
Few drops green food coloring
½ cup whipping cream
1 29-ounce can pear halves,
drained and diced
½ cup flaked coconut
Lettuce

Blend together cream cheese, sour cream, limeade concentrate, sugar, and food coloring. Whip cream till soft peaks form; fold into cream cheese mixture along with pears and coconut. Spread in 8×8×2-inch pan. Cover and freeze till firm. To serve, let stand at room temperature for 10 minutes. Cut in squares; serve on lettuce-lined salad plates. Garnish with additional whipped cream and coconut, if desired. Makes 9 servings.

Frozen Cranberry Salads

⅓ cup sugar
2 tablespoons cornstarch
Dash salt
1¼ cups cranberry-apple drink
2 slightly beaten egg yolks
1 10-ounce package frozen
cranberry-orange relish,
partially thawed
2 egg whites
⅓ cup instant nonfat dry milk
powder
Lettuce

In medium saucepan combine sugar, cornstarch, and salt; stir in *1 cup* of the cranberry-apple drink. Cook and stir over medium-high heat till thickened and bubbly. Remove from heat. Gradually stir about ½ of the hot mixture into egg yolks; return mixture to saucepan. Cook and stir 2 minutes more; stir in cranberry-orange relish. Cool mixture to room temperature.

In small mixer bowl combine egg whites, nonfat dry milk powder, and the remaining ¼ cup cranberry-apple drink. Beat till stiff peaks form; fold into egg yolk mixture. Spoon into 8 individual molds or paper bake-cup-lined muffin pans. Cover and freeze till firm. To serve, let stand at room temperature 10 minutes. Unmold, or peel off paper. Serve on lettuce-lined salad plates. Makes 8 servings.

3 MAIN DISH SALADS

If you're looking for a no fuss lunch or supper idea, a main dish salad is a natural. Choose one of these hearty salad bowl meals: *Asparagus and Shrimp Salad* (front, left), *Chicken and Brown Rice Toss* (back, left), *Chicken and Ham Supreme* (center), or *Pepper Steak Salad* (front, right). (See index for recipe pages.)

Hearty Main Dish Salads

Chef's Bowl (pictured above)

1 pound fresh asparagus
1 clove garlic, halved
1 medium head iceberg lettuce, torn (6 cups)
1 10-ounce package frozen peas, cooked, drained, and chilled
1 8-ounce package Swiss cheese, cut in julienne strips (2 cups)
5 to 8 ounces fully cooked ham, cut in julienne strips (1 to 1½ cups)
¾ cup sliced radishes
Salt
Pepper
Creamy French Dressing (see recipe, page 84)

Prepare asparagus according to directions in tip box on page 61. Drain and chill. Rub six individual salad bowls with cut garlic clove. Fill bowls with lettuce. Arrange asparagus, peas, cheese, ham, and radishes in bowls. Season to taste with some salt and pepper. Serve with *Creamy French Dressing*. Makes 6 servings.

Pepper Steak Salad (pictured on page 59)

1 pound cooked roast beef
2 small tomatoes
1 large green pepper
1 cup sliced celery
⅓ cup sliced green onion
⅓ cup sliced fresh mushrooms
½ cup bottled teriyaki sauce
⅓ cup dry sherry
⅓ cup salad oil
3 tablespoons white vinegar
½ teaspoon ground ginger
1 cup bean sprouts (see Mini Sprouting Garden recipe, page 90)
4 cups shredded Chinese cabbage

Cut cooked beef into thin strips; they should measure about 3 cups. Cut tomatoes into wedges and green pepper into strips. In mixing bowl combine beef, tomatoes, green pepper, celery, onion, and mushrooms. To make marinade, in screw-top jar combine teriyaki sauce, sherry, oil, vinegar, and ginger; shake well. Pour over beef mixture. Toss to coat well. Cover and refrigerate 2 to 3 hours. Add bean sprouts; toss again. Drain, reserving marinade. Place shredded Chinese cabbage in large salad bowl; top with marinated meat and vegetables. Pass reserved marinade for dressing. Makes 6 servings.

Asparagus and Shrimp Salad (pictured on page 58)

3 medium tomatoes
1 medium lemon
16 ounces fresh *or* frozen shrimp, shelled and cleaned
1 to 1½ pounds fresh asparagus
¼ cup sliced green onion
2 tablespoons snipped parsley
Fresh Herb Dressing (see recipe, page 83)
Lettuce

Cut tomatoes into wedges and lemon into thin slices; set aside. Cook fresh shrimp in large amount of boiling salted water for 1 to 3 minutes. (Cook frozen shrimp according to package directions.) Drain and set aside. Prepare asparagus according to tip box below, cutting spears into 1½-inch pieces. In mixing bowl combine shrimp, asparagus, lemon slices, onion, and parsley. Pour *Fresh Herb Dressing* over shrimp and vegetables. Cover and chill, stirring once or twice. To serve, drain vegetables and toss with tomato wedges; pile into lettuce-lined bowl. Makes 4 servings.

Fresh Asparagus: Buying, Storing, and Using

You'll find fresh asparagus available in most markets from mid-February through June. Frozen asparagus can be substituted during the off-season. Choose firm, straight stalks with tight, compact tips. Wrap stem ends in moist paper toweling; place in plastic bag or covered container and refrigerate. Use within 1 to 2 days.

To prepare asparagus, wash stalks and scrape off scales. Break off woody bases at point where stalks snap easily.

To cook, place whole spears in small amount of boiling salted water. To avoid overcooking, prop tips out of water with crumpled foil. Cook, covered, 10 minutes or till crisp-tender. Cook cut-up asparagus 8 to 10 minutes. Drain.

Beef and Caesar Salad (opposite, above)

1 egg
⅔ cup salad oil
1 3-ounce package cream cheese, softened
¼ cup dairy sour cream
2 tablespoons crumbled blue cheese
1 tablespoon lemon juice
2 teaspoons anchovy paste
¼ teaspoon garlic salt
8 ounces cooked roast beef
1 cup cherry tomatoes
4 cups torn romaine
2 cups torn fresh spinach
2 cups torn bibb lettuce
1 cup Garlic Croutons (see recipe, page 91)

To make dressing, in small mixer bowl beat egg slightly. Gradually add oil, beating at medium speed of electric mixer. Add cream cheese, sour cream, blue cheese, lemon juice, anchovy paste, and garlic salt; beat smooth. Cover and chill.

Cut beef into thin strips; season with a little salt. Halve cherry tomatoes. In large salad bowl combine romaine, spinach, bibb lettuce, *Garlic Croutons,* tomatoes, and beef; spoon about 1 cup dressing atop. Top with additional crumbled blue cheese, if desired. Toss to coat vegetables. Makes 6 servings.

Chili Salad (opposite, below)

1 medium head lettuce, cut in chunks
3 cups corn chips
1 large tomato, chopped
4 ounces pepperoni, thinly sliced
¼ cup pitted ripe olives
½ cup shredded cheddar cheese (2 ounces)
1 15-ounce can chili con carne with beans

In salad bowl combine lettuce, corn chips, chopped tomato, pepperoni, olives, and cheese. Meanwhile, in saucepan heat canned chili till bubbly. Immediately pour atop salad, tossing lightly to coat. Makes 6 servings.

Peachy Beef Toss

8 ounces cooked roast beef
4 cups torn romaine
3 cups torn fresh spinach
3 medium peaches, peeled, pitted, and sliced (1½ cups)
1 avocado, peeled, pitted, and sliced
12 cherry tomatoes, halved
½ cup salad oil
3 tablespoons vinegar
1 tablespoon prepared horseradish
½ teaspoon worcestershire sauce
Few drops bottled hot pepper sauce

Cut beef into julienne strips, according to directions in tip box on page 65. In salad bowl combine romaine, spinach, peaches, avocado, tomatoes, and roast beef strips. To make dressing, in screw-top jar combine salad oil, vinegar, horseradish, worcestershire sauce, bottled hot pepper sauce, ½ teaspoon *salt,* and ⅛ teaspoon *pepper.* Cover and shake well to mix. Pour dressing atop salad; toss to coat meat and vegetables. Makes 6 servings.

Top this great combo of salad greens and roast beef strips with a tangy dressing, cherry tomatoes, and croutons. *Beef and Caesar Salad* is a delicious meal in itself.

Quick-fixin' *Chili Salad* tastes like a meal-size taco in a bowl. Gently toss the salad with hot chili con carne to get that zesty, south-of-the-border taste.

Start with julienne strips of ham and chicken atop lettuce and vegetables for hearty *Mexican Chef's Salad*. Then pour a zesty, hot cheese sauce atop and sprinkle with corn chips.

Mexican Chef's Salad (opposite)

6 ounces cooked chicken
5 ounces fully cooked ham
1 medium head iceberg lettuce, torn (6 cups)
1 cup shredded carrot
1 cup chopped celery
2 medium tomatoes, chopped
3 tablespoons sliced green onion
2 cups shredded sharp American cheese (8 ounces)
⅔ cup milk
3 tablespoons chopped canned green chili peppers
3 tablespoons sliced pitted ripe olives
2 cups corn chips

Cut cooked chicken and ham into julienne strips, according to directions in tip box below (makes about 1 cup each of cut-up meat). In large salad bowl combine lettuce, carrot, and celery. Arrange tomatoes, green onion, chicken, and ham atop. In heavy saucepan combine cheese and milk. Cook over low heat, stirring constantly, till cheese is melted and mixture is smooth. Stir in chopped chilies and sliced olives. To serve, pour cheese mixture over salad. Toss lightly. Pass corn chips to sprinkle atop each serving. Makes 6 servings.

Chicken and Ham Supreme (pictured on page 58)

6 ounces cooked chicken
5 ounces fully cooked ham
2 medium tomatoes
1 medium green pepper
1 medium head iceberg lettuce, torn (6 cups)
1 cup sliced cucumber
3 hard-cooked eggs, sliced
½ cup salad oil
3 tablespoons vinegar
1 tablespoon prepared horseradish
½ teaspoon worcestershire sauce
Few drops bottled hot pepper sauce
½ teaspoon salt
⅛ teaspoon pepper

Cut cooked chicken and ham into julienne strips, according to directions in tip box below (makes about 1 cup each of cut-up meat). Cut tomatoes into wedges; cut green pepper into narrow strips. Fill four individual salad bowls with the lettuce. Arrange cucumber, eggs, chicken, ham, tomatoes, and green pepper in each bowl. To make dressing, in screw-top jar combine oil, vinegar, horseradish, worcestershire sauce, hot pepper sauce, salt, and pepper. Cover and shake well to mix. Pass dressing with salads. Makes 4 servings.

How to "Julienne"

"Julienne" meats and vegetables by cutting into long thin strips. First cut a thin slice off one side of the meat or vegetable, if necessary, to make it lie flat on the cutting board. Placing flat side down, cut into thin lengthwise slices. Then cut each slice into narrow strips about ⅛- to ¼-inch thick.

Tuna Salad in Tomato Cups (opposite, above)

1 6½- *or* 7-ounce can tuna, drained and flaked
½ cup sliced celery
¼ cup sliced pimiento-stuffed olives
¼ cup sliced green onion
1 tablespoon lemon juice
¼ teaspoon salt
Dash pepper
2 hard-cooked eggs, chopped
½ cup mayonnaise *or* salad dressing
4 medium tomatoes
Lettuce

In mixing bowl combine tuna, celery, olives, green onion, lemon juice, salt, and pepper. Gently stir in chopped egg and mayonnaise or salad dressing; cover and chill.

Prepare tomato cups according to directions in tip box on page 79. To serve, place chilled tomatoes on individual lettuce-lined plates; sprinkle with salt. Fill each tomato cup with about ½ cup of the tuna mixture. Garnish with parsley, olives, or additional hard-cooked egg slices, if desired. Makes 4 servings.

Avocado Egg Salad (opposite, below left)

4 hard-cooked eggs, chopped
4 slices bacon, crisp-cooked, drained, and crumbled
1 tablespoon finely chopped green onion
2 large avocados, halved and seeded
Lemon juice
2 tablespoons mayonnaise *or* salad dressing
2 teaspoons lemon juice
1 teaspoon prepared mustard
½ teaspoon salt
Dash pepper
Lettuce

In small mixing bowl combine eggs, bacon, and onion. Carefully scoop out avocado halves, leaving firm shells; brush shells with a little lemon juice to prevent browning. Mash avocado pulp. In mixing bowl stir together the mayonnaise, 2 teaspoons lemon juice, mustard, salt, and pepper. Add mashed avocado and the egg mixture; spoon avocado-egg salad mixture into avocado shells. Place filled avocados on individual lettuce-lined serving plates. Garnish with bacon curl, if desired. Makes 2 servings.

Lobster in Orange Cups (opposite, below right)

4 large oranges
1 5-ounce can lobster *or* 1¼ cups cooked lobster, broken into pieces
1 cup thinly sliced celery
¼ cup mayonnaise *or* salad dressing
¼ teaspoon salt
Leaf lettuce
2 teaspoons thinly sliced green onion

Cut slice from top of each orange. Remove fruit from oranges, leaving shells. Discard orange tops. Chop fruit. Cut top edge of each orange shell in sawtooth fashion. Place orange shells in plastic bag and refrigerate. In mixing bowl combine chopped orange, lobster, and celery; chill.

Stir together mayonnaise or salad dressing and salt. Drain lobster mixture; add to mayonnaise mixture and toss. Line 4 orange shells with lettuce; spoon in lobster mixture. Place filled orange cups on lettuce-lined plates. Garnish orange cups with sliced green onion. Makes 4 servings.

Tuna Salad in Tomato Cups, nestled on a bed of frilly leaf lettuce, is an easy
way to dress up everyday ingredients. For added color, garnish with pimiento-stuffed olive slices.

Add avocado and bacon to the popular salad
sandwich filling for elegant *Avocado Egg Salad*.

For the light appetite, citrus and
seafood team up in *Lobster in Orange Cups*.

Crab-Stuffed Avocados (pictured on cover)

1 **pound crab legs, cooked, chilled, and shelled (½ pound crab meat),** *or* 1 **7-ounce can crab meat, chilled and drained**
2 **hard-cooked eggs, chopped**
¼ **cup chopped celery**
¼ **cup mayonnaise** *or* **salad dressing**
1 **teaspoon dry mustard**
¼ **teaspoon salt**
 Dash worcestershire sauce
4 **medium avocados**

Break crab meat into pieces; set aside several larger segments of meat. Combine remaining crab meat with eggs, celery, mayonnaise or salad dressing, mustard, salt, and worcestershire sauce. Chill. Prepare avocado shells according to directions in tip box below. Fill avocados with crab mixture. Top with pieces of reserved crab meat. Serve on lettuce-lined plates, if desired. Makes 4 servings.

Chicken Salad a l'Orange

12 **ounces cooked chicken, cubed (2 cups)**
1 **cup sliced celery**
½ **cup sliced pitted ripe olives**
3 **tablespoons frozen orange juice concentrate, thawed**
3 **tablespoons salad oil**
1 **tablespoon sugar**
1 **tablespoon vinegar**
⅛ **teaspoon dry mustard**
 Few drops bottled hot pepper sauce
¼ **cup mayonnaise** *or* **salad dressing**
1 **medium avocado**
1 **medium orange**

In mixing bowl combine chicken, celery, and olives; cover and chill. To make dressing, stir together orange juice concentrate, oil, sugar, vinegar, dry mustard, hot pepper sauce, and dash *salt*. Fold in mayonnaise or salad dressing. Pour over chicken mixture and toss lightly to coat. Cover and chill. Pit, peel, and slice avocado according to tip box below. Peel and section orange. Arrange avocado slices and orange sections on individual serving plates. Mound chicken mixture in center. Makes 3 or 4 servings.

Avocados

Avocados range in color from green to almost black, but the ripeness test is the same for all varieties. The fruit should yield to gentle pressure when ready to eat. Store firm avocados at room temperature to ripen quickly; refrigerate to ripen slowly.

To prepare avocados, cut fruit in half lengthwise; twist gently and separate. Tap seed with sharp edge of knife; twist and lift or gently pry out seed. Use a knife to loosen and strip skin from fruit. (The peel may be left on for filled avocado shells.)

To make avocado rest firmly, trim a thin slice from bottom of each half. Fill avocado half with salad mixture or slice to use in tossed salads. Brush cut surface of avocado with lemon juice to prevent darkening.

Polynesian Shrimp Bowl

1 15¼-ounce can pineapple
   chunks (juice pack)
2 teaspoons cornstarch
1½ teaspoons curry powder
2 teaspoons lemon juice
⅓ cup mayonnaise *or* salad
   dressing
⅓ cup dairy sour cream
2 cups medium noodles,
   cooked, drained,
   and chilled
2 4½-ounce cans shrimp,
   rinsed and drained
½ cup sliced water chestnuts
¼ cup chopped green pepper

Drain pineapple, reserving juice. Set pineapple aside. To make curry dressing; in small saucepan combine cornstarch, curry powder, reserved pineapple juice, and ¼ teaspoon *salt*. Cook and stir over medium heat till thick and bubbly; stir in lemon juice. Cool. Blend in mayonnaise and sour cream. In salad bowl combine pineapple chunks, noodles, shrimp, water chestnuts, and green pepper. Pour on curry dressing; toss gently to coat. Chill thoroughly. Makes 6 servings.

Chicken and Brown Rice Toss (pictured on page 58)

3 cups cooked brown rice
12 ounces cooked chicken,
   cubed (2 cups)
½ cup sliced celery
¼ cup sliced pitted ripe
   olives
2 tablespoons sliced green
   onion
½ cup mayonnaise *or* salad
   dressing
¼ cup Italian salad dressing
½ cup coarsely chopped
   cashew nuts
   Lettuce

In mixing bowl combine cooked brown rice, chicken, celery, olives, and green onion. Stir together mayonnaise and Italian dressing; add to chicken mixture. Toss gently to coat. Cover and chill. Just before serving, add cashews and toss again. Turn into lettuce-lined salad bowl. Makes 4 or 5 servings.

Quick Tuna-Macaroni Salad

1 16-ounce can macaroni and
   cheese
1 8-ounce can peas, drained
1 6½- *or* 7-ounce can tuna,
   drained and flaked
2 hard-cooked eggs, chopped
¼ cup mayonnaise *or* salad
   dressing
1 tablespoon finely chopped
   green pepper
1 teaspoon prepared mustard
1 teaspoon minced dried
   onion
6 medium tomatoes
   Lettuce
   Paprika

In mixing bowl combine macaroni and cheese, peas, tuna, eggs, mayonnaise or salad dressing, green pepper, mustard, onion, ¼ teaspoon *salt,* and dash *pepper*. Cover and chill. Prepare tomato cups according to directions on page 79. To serve, place tomato cups on individual lettuce-lined plates; fill with tuna mixture. Sprinkle with paprika. Makes 6 servings.

Sausage Supper Salad (opposite)

4 cups torn iceberg lettuce
8 ounces assorted dry and
   semi-dry sausages
2 hard-cooked eggs, cut in
   wedges
½ of a 15-ounce can (1 cup)
   garbanzo beans, drained
1 cup sliced celery
½ cup chopped onion
½ cup mayonnaise
2 tablespoons milk
1½ teaspoons prepared
   horseradish
½ teaspoon dry mustard

Place lettuce in a large bowl. Cut sausages in thin slices, then in bite-size pieces. Arrange sausages, egg wedges, beans, celery, and onion atop lettuce. To make dressing, blend together mayonnaise, milk, horseradish, and mustard; pour over salad. Toss to coat vegetables and sausages. Makes 4 to 6 servings.

Salami-Cheese Salad

1 medium head iceberg
   lettuce, torn (6 cups)
5 ounces salami, sliced
   and quartered (1 cup)
4 ounces Swiss cheese, cut
   in strips
½ cup sliced pitted ripe
   olives
3 tablespoons chopped
   pimiento
¾ cup Italian Dressing (see
   recipe, page 83)

In salad bowl combine lettuce, salami, cheese, olives, and pimiento. Pour *Italian Dressing* over salad and toss lightly. Makes 4 servings.

Cassoulet Salad

2 16-ounce cans red kidney
   beans, drained
1 16-ounce can pinto beans,
   drained
1 15-ounce can garbanzo
   beans, drained
¼ cup sliced green onion
1 2-ounce jar (¼ cup)
   pimiento, chopped
½ of a 15½-ounce jar (1 cup)
   spaghetti sauce
⅓ cup white wine vinegar
2 tablespoons salad oil
   Few dashes bottled hot
   pepper sauce
6 cups torn mixed salad
   greens
4 ounces thuringer sausage,
   sliced

In large bowl combine kidney beans, pinto beans, garbanzo beans, onion, and pimiento. To make dressing, in small bowl combine spaghetti sauce, wine vinegar, salad oil, and hot pepper sauce; pour over bean mixture. Cover; refrigerate several hours or overnight, stirring occasionally. In salad bowl combine torn greens, sausage, and bean mixture. Toss. Makes 12 servings.

An assortment of sausages such as salami, pepperoni, and mortadella add variety to
Sausage Supper Salad. This main dish salad gets added protein from garbanzo beans and eggs.

Caesar's Chicken Salad (opposite, above)

3 anchovy fillets
¼ cup salad oil *or* olive oil
½ teaspoon dry mustard
2 tablespoons lemon juice
1 teaspoon worcestershire
   sauce
1 egg
12 ounces cooked chicken
1 7-ounce can artichoke
   hearts, drained
4 cups torn romaine
½ cup Garlic Croutons (see
   recipe, page 91)
2 tablespoons grated par-
   mesan cheese

To make dressing, cream together anchovies, *1 tablespoon* of the oil, dry mustard, and a dash *pepper*. Blend in lemon juice, worcestershire, and remaining oil; set aside. To coddle egg, place whole egg in small saucepan of boiling water; immediately remove from heat and let stand 1 minute. Remove egg from water; cool slightly. Break egg into dressing mixture. Beat till dressing becomes creamy. Cut chicken in julienne strips according to directions in tip box on page 65. Halve artichoke hearts. In large salad bowl combine chicken, artichokes, romaine, *Garlic Croutons*, and parmesan. Pour dressing over and toss to coat. Makes 6 servings.

Curried Chicken Salad (opposite, below)

1 large orange
1 medium banana
4 cups torn mixed salad
   greens
12 ounces cooked chicken,
   cubed (2 cups)
½ of an 8-ounce can (½ cup)
   jellied cranberry sauce,
   chilled and cut in ½-
   inch cubes
¼ cup light raisins
¼ cup salted peanuts
½ cup mayonnaise *or* salad
   dressing
½ of an 8-ounce carton (½
   cup) orange yogurt
½ to 1 teaspoon curry powder

Section orange over bowl to catch juice. Slice banana diagonally and dip in reserved orange juice. Place salad greens in large salad bowl. Arrange orange sections, banana, chicken, the cranberry cubes, raisins, and peanuts atop salad greens. Chill. To make dressing, combine mayonnaise or salad dressing, yogurt, and curry; chill. Pass dressing with salad. Makes 4 servings.

Imperial Chicken Salad

12 ounces cooked chicken,
   cut in strips (2 cups)
4 medium potatoes, cooked,
   peeled, and sliced
3 hard-cooked eggs, sliced
½ cup chopped dill pickle
½ cup chopped celery
1 tablespoon grated onion
1 tablespoon capers, drained
   and rinsed
¾ cup mayonnaise *or* salad
   dressing
1 tablespoon lemon juice

In large bowl combine chicken, potatoes, sliced eggs, pickle, celery, onion, capers, and 1 teaspoon *salt*. Blend together mayonnaise or salad dressing and lemon juice; stir mayonnaise mixture into salad. Chill. To serve, mound salad on plate. Garnish top with sieved hard-cooked egg, if desired. Makes 6 servings.

The traditional anchovy-egg Caesar dressing is tossed with romaine, chicken, and artichoke hearts for an upbeat main dish, *Caesar's Chicken Salad.*

Orange, banana, cranberry sauce cubes, raisins, peanuts, and a spicy yogurt dressing give an exotic flavor to *Curried Chicken Salad.*

Calorie-counted Salads

Marinated Tuna and Vegetables (pictured above)

2 large carrots, cut in
  julienne strips
1½ cups cauliflowerets
1 10-ounce package frozen
  peas
1 6½- or 7-ounce can tuna
½ cup thinly sliced celery
¼ cup sliced green onion
¾ cup Zesty Salad Dressing
  (see recipe, page 88)

Cook carrots and cauliflower together, uncovered, in small amount of boiling salted water for 10 minutes. Add peas. Cook 5 minutes more or till all vegetables are crisp-tender. Drain. Drain tuna well. In mixing bowl combine cooked vegetables, celery, and green onion. Add tuna and *Zesty Salad Dressing;* toss gently to coat. Cover and chill. Serve on lettuce leaf, if desired. Makes 3 servings (224 calories per serving).

Confetti Chicken Salad

12 ounces cooked chicken
  white meat, diced
  (2 cups)
1 cup chopped celery
½ cup shredded carrot
½ cup alfalfa sprouts (see
  Sprouting Mini Garden recipe,
  page 90)
½ cup Diet Salad Dressing
  (see recipe, page 89)
1 tablespoon lime juice

In bowl combine chicken, celery, carrot, and alfalfa sprouts. Stir together the *Diet Salad Dressing* and lime juice; pour over chicken mixture, tossing to coat. Makes 4 servings (124 calories per serving).

Salmon-Stuffed Tomatoes

1 9-ounce package frozen
  artichoke hearts
1 16-ounce can salmon,
  drained, boned, and
  broken into chunks
3 hard-cooked eggs, chopped
1 cup sliced fresh mushrooms
¼ teaspoon salt
6 large tomatoes
1 cup dairy sour cream
¼ cup diced cucumber
¼ cup milk
1 tablespoon lemon juice
2 teaspoons snipped fresh
  dillweed *or* ½ teaspoon
  dried dillweed
¼ teaspoon salt

Cook frozen artichoke hearts according to package directions; drain and chop. In mixing bowl combine chopped artichoke hearts, salmon, eggs, mushrooms, ¼ teaspoon salt, and dash *pepper;* cover and chill. Prepare tomato cups according to directions in tip box on page 79. Place tomato cups on serving plate; fill with salmon mixture. To make dressing combine sour cream, cucumber, milk, lemon juice, dill, and ¼ teaspoon salt. Pour dressing over filled tomato. Makes 6 servings (274 calories per serving).

Meatless Meal-in-a-Bowl

1 cup cherry tomatoes
4 cups torn fresh spinach
1 15-ounce can garbanzo
  beans, drained
1 cup cauliflowerets
1 cup sliced fresh mushrooms
1 small cucumber, sliced
½ small red onion, thinly
  sliced and separated
  into rings
½ cup coarsely chopped
  walnuts
1 small avocado
1 8-ounce carton (1 cup)
  plain yogurt
¼ cup milk
1 tablespoon honey
¼ teaspoon garlic salt

Halve cherry tomatoes. In salad bowl combine tomatoes, spinach, beans, cauliflower, mushrooms, cucumber, onion rings, and walnuts.
  To make dressing peel, seed, and cut up avocado (see tip box on page 68). In blender container combine avocado, yogurt, milk, honey, and garlic salt. Cover and blend till mixture is smooth. Add additional milk if needed to make desired consistency. Pour dressing over salad; toss to coat. Makes 4 servings (316 calories per serving).

Chicken Pineapple Boat

12 ounces cooked chicken,
  cubed (2 cups)
1 15¼-ounce can pineapple
  chunks (juice pack), chilled
  and drained
1 medium green pepper, cut
  in strips
½ cup sliced water chestnuts
¾ cup Zesty Salad Dressing
  (see recipe, page 88)

In salad bowl combine chicken, pineapple, green pepper, and water chestnuts. Pour *Zesty Salad Dressing* over chicken mixture; toss lightly. Makes 4 servings (201 calories per serving).

Turkey in Aspic (opposite, above)

12 ounces cooked turkey white meat, cut in 6 slices
4 hard-cooked eggs, sliced
¾ pound fresh *or* 1 8-ounce package frozen asparagus spears, cooked and drained
6 pimiento strips
2 envelopes unflavored gelatin
2 13¾-ounce cans chicken broth
½ cup water
1 thin slice onion
2 tablespoons lemon juice
2 teaspoons prepared horse-radish
1 sprig parsley

Trim turkey slices to uniform shapes; arrange in 13×9×2-inch pan. Top each with 4 egg slices, about 3 asparagus spears, and a pimiento strip. In medium saucepan soften gelatin in chicken broth and water. Add onion, lemon juice, horseradish, and parsley. Bring to boiling, stirring frequently. Remove from heat and strain through cheesecloth. Chill just till syrupy. Spoon a little of the broth mixture over each salad in pan. Chill till almost set; keep remaining broth mixture at room temperature and stir occasionally. Repeat, spooning room-temperature broth mixture over turkey slices and chilling till a thin glaze of gelatin forms. Pour remaining broth mixture around salads in pan. Chill till set. To serve, trim around each turkey slice and transfer to serving plates. Break up remaining gelatin in pan with a fork and arrange around salads on serving plates. Makes 6 servings (206 calories per serving).

Shrimp Tomato Vinaigrette (opposite, below left)

2 cups cleaned cooked shrimp
1 6-ounce package frozen pea pods, thawed
2 tablespoons sliced green onion
¼ cup salad oil
2 tablespoons dry white wine
2 tablespoons white vinegar
1 0.6-ounce envelope Italian salad dressing mix
1 to 2 teaspoons capers, drained
Dash pepper
4 tomatoes

In mixing bowl combine shrimp, pea pods, and onion. To make dressing, in screw-top jar combine oil, wine, vinegar, Italian salad dressing mix, capers, and pepper; cover and shake well to mix. Pour dressing over shrimp mixture. Cover and refrigerate several hours. Prepare tomato cups according to directions on page 79. To serve, drain shrimp mixture; spoon into tomato cups. Place on lettuce-lined plates, if desired. Makes 4 servings (210 calories per serving).

Salmon Potato Salad (opposite, below right)

3 medium potatoes, cooked, peeled, and cubed (3 cups)
1 hard-cooked egg, chopped
½ cup sliced celery
½ cup shredded carrot
2 tablespoons chopped green onion
Cottage Dressing
1 16-ounce can salmon, drained, boned, and broken into chunks
Green pepper rings

In large bowl combine potatoes, egg, celery, carrot, and onion. Add Cottage Dressing to potato mixture, tossing lightly to coat. Gently fold in salmon. Cover and chill thoroughly. Place atop green pepper rings on individual salad plates; garnish with carrot curls and additional green pepper, if desired. Makes 6 servings (285 calories per serving).

Cottage Dressing: Blend together 1 cup cream-style *cottage cheese*, ½ cup *mayonnaise or salad dressing*, 2 tablespoons *milk*, 2 tablespoons *lemon juice*, 1 teaspoon dried *dillweed*, ¼ teaspoon *salt*, and a dash *pepper*.

For special luncheon menus, prepare individual servings of *Turkey in Aspic*.
These elegant, gelatin-glazed salad entrées go easy on calories but not on flavor.

A light vinegar-and-oil dressing flavors
the filling for *Shrimp Tomato Vinaigrette*.

For a low-calorie supper, turn a summer side
dish into protein-packed *Salmon Potato Salad*.

Salad Burritos

1 8-ounce can garbanzo *or* red kidney beans
½ small onion, sliced and separated into rings
½ cup sliced pitted ripe olives
½ cup salad oil
½ of a 1.25-ounce envelope (3 tablespoons) taco seasoning mix
3 tablespoons vinegar
½ teaspoon sugar
4 cups torn iceberg lettuce
8 ounces monterey jack cheese, cut in strips (2 cups)
1 small sweet red *or* green pepper, cut in strips
12 8-inch flour tortillas

Drain beans. In mixing bowl combine beans, onion rings, and olives. To make dressing, in screw-top jar combine salad oil, taco seasoning mix, vinegar, and sugar. Cover and shake well. Pour over bean mixture. Cover and chill. Just before serving, add lettuce, cheese, and pepper strips to marinated bean mixture. Toss gently to coat. Spoon about ½ cup salad atop each tortilla; roll up, folding in sides. Makes 6 servings (458 calories per serving).

Slim Ham Slaw

2 tablespoons all-purpose flour
2 tablespoons sugar
1 teaspoon salt
1 teaspoon dry mustard
½ teaspoon celery seed
1 cup skim milk
2 slightly beaten egg yolks
3 tablespoons vinegar
2 tablespoons lemon juice
6 cups coarsely shredded cabbage
10 ounces fully cooked ham, cubed (2½ cups)
1 medium apple, cored and chopped (1 cup)
¼ cup chopped green pepper

For dressing, in small saucepan combine flour, sugar, salt, dry mustard, and celery seed; gradually blend in milk. Cook and stir over medium heat till thickened and bubbly. Stir a moderate amount of hot mixture into egg yolks; return all to saucepan. Cook and stir over low heat 1 to 2 minutes more or till thickened. Stir in vinegar and lemon juice; cool. Combine cabbage, ham, apple, and green pepper. Toss with dressing mixture; cover and chill. Makes 4 servings (260 calories per serving).

Cottage Cabbage Apple Slaw

2 cups shredded cabbage
1 medium apple, cored and chopped
½ cup Diet Blue Cheese Dressing (see recipe, page 89)
1 12-ounce carton (1½ cups) cream-style cottage cheese

In salad bowl combine cabbage and apple. Pour *Diet Blue Cheese Dressing* over cabbage mixture; toss to coat. Spoon cottage cheese in ring around edge of salad bowl. Makes 4 servings (144 calories per serving).

Sprout Salad

2 cups alfalfa sprouts
  (see Sprouting Mini
  Garden recipe,
  page 90)
1 medium tomato
¼ cup sliced green onion
¼ cup snipped parsley
2 tablespoons chopped green
  pepper
  Garlic Dressing
1 cup cubed cheddar cheese

Cook sprouts, uncovered, in small amount of boiling water for 3 minutes; drain and cool. Peel and chop the tomato. In mixing bowl combine sprouts, tomato, onion, parsley, and green pepper. Pour Garlic Dressing over sprouts mixture and toss gently to coat. Cover and chill 30 minutes. Add cheese and mix lightly. Serve in lettuce cups, if desired. Makes 4 servings (316 calories per serving).

Garlic Dressing: In screw-top jar combine 3 tablespoons *salad oil,* 2 tablespoons *wine vinegar,* ⅛ teaspoon *garlic salt,* and a dash freshly ground *pepper.* Cover; shake well.

Grapefruit-Seafood Salad

1 7-ounce can water-pack tuna
2 grapefruit, peeled
4 cups shredded lettuce
½ cup chopped celery
½ cup Tomato Salad Dressing
  (see recipe, page 89)

Drain tuna; break into chunks. Section grapefruit. Combine tuna, grapefruit, lettuce, and celery. Toss with *Tomato Salad Dressing.* Makes 4 servings (122 calories per serving).

Cottage Cheese Bean Sprout Salad

2 medium tomatoes
1 cup cream-style cottage
  cheese
1 cup mung bean sprouts
  (see Sprouting Mini
  Garden recipe, page 90)
½ cup chopped cucumber
2 tablespoons sliced green
  onion
¼ teaspoon salt

Prepare tomato cups according to instructions in tip box below.

In mixing bowl combine cottage cheese, bean sprouts chopped cucumber, green onion, and salt. To serve, place chilled tomato cups on individual salad plates. Fill each tomato with *half* the cottage cheese mixture. Makes 2 servings (277 calories per serving).

Tomato Cups

Fresh, red-ripe tomatoes make attractive containers for individual servings of main dish salads. To make decorative petal cups as shown at left, place tomatoes, stem end down, on cutting surface. With sharp knife, cut tomato into 4 to 6 wedges, cutting to, but not through, the stem end of the tomato. Spread the wedges apart slightly; sprinkle lightly with salt. Cover and chill. When ready to serve, spread the wedges apart and spoon in the salad mixture.

To make plain cups, cut a small slice from the top of the tomato. Remove core, if present. Use a spoon to scoop out the seeds, leaving a ½-inch-thick shell. To dress up these cups, carefully cut the edge into scallops or a sawtooth pattern. Sprinkle the cups with salt. Invert and chill. Fill with salad at serving time.

4 SALAD DRESSERS

A bowl of fresh greens becomes an exciting salad when tossed with just the right dressing—the dressing determines the success of the salad. You can liven up a so-so salad by topping it with homemade croutons, fresh sprouts, or fresh vegetable garnishes. Try combining your favorite greens with these salad seasoners: *Sprouting Mini Garden* (front, left), *Fresh Herb Dressing* (back, left), *Diet Thousand Island Dressing* (back, center), *Garlic Croutons* (center, back), *Rye Croutons* (back, right), *Red Wine Dressing* (front, right). (See index for recipe pages.)

Shake-it-together Dressings

Tomato Soup Dressing (pictured above)

1 10¾-ounce can condensed
   tomato soup
¾ cup vinegar
½ cup salad oil
2 tablespoons sugar
2 teaspoons grated onion
2 teaspoons dry mustard
1½ teaspoons salt
1½ teaspoons worcestershire
   sauce
½ teaspoon paprika
¼ teaspoon garlic powder
   Dash cayenne

In blender container combine soup, vinegar, oil, sugar, grated onion, dry mustard, salt, worcestershire, paprika, garlic powder, and cayenne. Cover and blend till smooth. Transfer to storage container. Cover and chill. Shake again just before serving. Makes about 2⅓ cups.

Fresh Herb Dressing (pictured on page 80)

¼ cup salad oil
3 tablespoons dry white wine
2 tablespoons lemon juice
1 tablespoon sugar
1 tablespoon snipped fresh
   basil *or* 1 teaspoon
   dried basil, crushed
1 teaspoon salt
   Several dashes bottled
   hot pepper sauce

In screw-top jar combine oil, wine, lemon juice, sugar, basil, salt, bottled hot pepper sauce, and ¼ teaspoon *pepper*. Cover and shake to mix well. Chill. Shake again before serving. Makes ½ cup.

Red Wine Dressing (pictured on page 81)

1 cup salad oil
⅓ cup vinegar
⅓ cup dry red wine
1 teaspoon sugar
1 teaspoon dried thyme,
   crushed
½ teaspoon dried oregano,
   crushed
1 clove garlic

In screw-top jar combine oil, vinegar, wine, sugar, thyme, oregano, garlic, and ¼ teaspoon *salt*. Cover and shake to mix well. Chill. Remove garlic clove; shake again just before serving. Makes 1⅔ cups.

Italian Dressing

1⅓ cups salad oil
½ cup vinegar
¼ cup grated parmesan cheese
1 tablespoon sugar
2 teaspoons salt
1 teaspoon celery salt
½ teaspoon white pepper
½ teaspoon dry mustard
¼ teaspoon paprika
1 clove garlic, minced

In screw-top jar combine oil, vinegar, parmesan cheese, sugar, salt, celery salt, white pepper, dry mustard, paprika, and garlic. Cover and shake to mix well. Chill. Shake again just before serving. Makes 1¾ cups.

Russian Dressing

⅔ cup salad oil
½ cup catsup
¼ cup sugar
3 tablespoons lemon juice
2 tablespoons worcestershire
   sauce
2 tablespoons vinegar
2 tablespoons water
1 tablespoon grated onion
½ teaspoon salt
½ teaspoon paprika

In screw-top jar combine oil, catsup, sugar, lemon juice, worcestershire, vinegar, water, onion, salt, and paprika. Cover and shake to mix well. Chill. Shake again just before serving. Makes 1¾ cups.

Tangy Tomato Dressing

1 8-ounce can tomato sauce
1 tablespoon vinegar
1 teaspoon worcestershire
  sauce
1 teaspoon sugar
1 teaspoon grated onion
½ teaspoon prepared
  horseradish
½ teaspoon salt
  Few drops bottled hot
  pepper sauce

In screw-top jar combine tomato sauce, vinegar, worcestershire, sugar, onion, horseradish, salt, hot pepper sauce, and ⅛ teaspoon *pepper*. Cover and shake to mix well. Chill. Shake again just before serving. Makes 1 cup.

Zesty Blue Cheese Dressing

¾ cup salad oil
¼ cup lemon juice
2 tablespoons sliced green
  onion
2 tablespoons snipped parsley
1 tablespoon dijon-style
  mustard
1 teaspoon sugar
¼ teaspoon garlic salt
⅓ cup crumbled blue cheese

In screw-top jar combine oil, lemon juice, onion, parsley, mustard, sugar, garlic salt, and a dash *pepper*. Cover and shake well to mix. Chill. Add blue cheese and shake again just before serving. Makes 1½ cups.

Creamy French Dressing

1 tablespoon paprika
2 teaspoons sugar
1 teaspoon salt
  Dash cayenne
¼ cup vinegar
1 egg
1 cup salad oil

In small mixer bowl combine paprika, sugar, salt, and cayenne. Add vinegar and egg; beat well. Add salad oil in slow, steady stream, beating constantly with electric mixer or rotary beater till thick. Transfer to storage container. Cover and chill. Makes about 1⅔ cups.

Chili Dressing

½ cup salad oil
3 tablespoons vinegar
3 tablespoons lemon juice
3 tablespoons chili sauce
1 tablespoon grated onion
2 teaspoons sugar
1½ teaspoons chili powder
¾ teaspoon dry mustard
½ teaspoon salt
⅛ teaspoon paprika
  Few dashes bottled hot
  pepper sauce

In screw-top jar combine oil, vinegar, lemon juice, chili sauce, grated onion, sugar, chili powder, dry mustard, salt, paprika, and hot pepper sauce. Cover and shake well to mix. Chill. Shake again just before serving. Makes 1 cup.

Vinaigrette with Variations

This classic French dressing is a thin, clear vinegar and oil mixture used to dress or marinate vegetables, salads, meats, or fish. Create a flavor to suit your taste by varying the oil, acid, and seasonings used. Here's the basic formula for

Vinaigrette Dressing: In screw-top jar combine oil, acid, sweetener, salt, and choice of seasonings. Cover and shake well to mix. Chill. Shake again just before serving. Makes about 1½ cups. Store unused dressing in refrigerator up to one month.

OIL	(salad oil, olive oil, or a combination of both)	1 cup
ACID	(vinegar, lemon or lime juice, or combination)	⅔ cup
SWEETENER	(sugar, corn syrup, or honey)	1 to 2 teaspoons
SALT		1½ teaspoons
DRY MUSTARD	(optional)	1½ teaspoons
PAPRIKA	(optional)	1½ teaspoons
HERBS	(thyme, oregano, basil, tarragon, dillweed, chives)	2 to 3 teaspoons snipped fresh *or* ½ to 1 teaspoon dried, crushed

Tailored for Fruit Salads

This smooth, sweet dressing is the perfect topper for fresh or canned fruits and is especially good with the tart contrast of citrus fruit salads. Vary the ingredients to suit your taste, following the chart below for Sweet Seed Dressing: In small mixer

bowl combine sweetener, paprika, dry mustard, and salt. Stir in acid. Add oil in slow, steady stream, beating constantly with electric mixer or rotary beater till thick. Beat in choice of seed. Cover and chill. Makes 1¾ cups.

SWEETENER	(sugar, corn syrup, or honey)	⅔ cup
PAPRIKA		1 teaspoon
DRY MUSTARD		1 teaspoon
SALT		¼ teaspoon
ACID	(vinegar, lemon or lime juice, or combination)	⅓ cup
SALAD OIL		1 cup
SEED	(celery, poppy, or toasted sesame seed)	1 to 2 teaspoons

Dairy Salad Dressings

Cucumber Cream Dressing (pictured above)

½ cup finely chopped unpeeled
   cucumber
2 tablespoons finely chopped
   green pepper
2 tablespoons thinly sliced
   green onion
2 tablespoons thinly sliced
   radishes
1 cup dairy sour cream
2 tablespoons milk
½ teaspoon salt
   Dash pepper

In mixing bowl combine cucumber, green pepper, onion, and radishes. Stir in sour cream, milk, salt, and pepper; mix well. Transfer to storage container. Cover and chill. Garnish with additional radish slices and a sprig of fresh watercress, if desired. Makes 1½ cups.

Green Goddess Dressing

¾ cup snipped parsley
½ cup mayonnaise *or* salad
   dressing
½ cup dairy sour cream
1 green onion, cut up
2 tablespoons tarragon
   vinegar
1 tablespoon anchovy paste
½ teaspoon dried basil,
   crushed
¼ teaspoon sugar

In blender container combine parsley, mayonnaise or salad dressing, sour cream, green onion, vinegar, anchovy paste, basil, and sugar. Cover and blend till smooth. Transfer to storage container. Cover and chill. Makes 1¼ cups.

Blue Cheese Salad Dressing

1 cup mayonnaise *or* salad
   dressing
1 small onion, cut up
⅓ cup salad oil
¼ cup catsup
2 tablespoons sugar
2 tablespoons vinegar
1 teaspoon prepared mustard
½ teaspoon paprika
¼ teaspoon celery seed
1 cup crumbled blue cheese

In blender container combine mayonnaise or salad dressing, onion, salad oil, catsup, sugar, vinegar, mustard, paprika, celery seed, ½ teaspoon *salt,* and dash *pepper.* Cover and blend till smooth. Transfer dressing to storage container; stir in blue cheese. Cover and chill. Makes 2½ cups.

Buttermilk Dressing

½ cup mayonnaise *or* salad
   dressing
½ cup chive-style sour cream dip
½ cup buttermilk
¼ cup tomato juice
2 tablespoons grated parmesan
   cheese
½ teaspoon dry mustard
¼ teaspoon paprika
¼ teaspoon celery seed
⅛ teaspoon garlic powder

In a bowl blend mayonnaise or salad dressing, sour cream dip, buttermilk, tomato juice, parmesan cheese, dry mustard, paprika, celery seed, garlic powder, ⅛ teaspoon *salt,* and ⅛ teaspoon *pepper.* Transfer to storage container. Cover and chill. Makes 1¾ cups.

Creamy Garlic Dressing

½ cup mayonnaise *or* salad
   dressing
½ cup Italian salad dressing
2 tablespoons finely shredded
   cheddar cheese
1 tablespoon anchovy paste

In mixing bowl blend together mayonnaise or salad dressing, Italian dressing, cheddar cheese, and anchovy paste; mix well. Transfer to storage container. Cover and chill. Makes 1 cup.

Waist-watcher Dressings

Zesty Salad Dressing (above, left)

- 1 tablespoon cornstarch
- 1 teaspoon sugar
- 1 teaspoon dry mustard
- 1 cup cold water
- ¼ cup vinegar
- ¼ cup catsup
- 1 teaspoon prepared horseradish
- 1 teaspoon worcestershire sauce
- ½ teaspoon salt
- ½ teaspoon paprika
  Dash bottled hot pepper sauce
- 1 clove garlic, halved

In a small saucepan combine the cornstarch, sugar, and the dry mustard; gradually stir in water. Cook, stirring constantly, over medium heat till thick and bubbly. Remove from heat. Cover surface with waxed paper. Cool 10 to 15 minutes. Remove waxed paper; stir in the vinegar, catsup, horseradish, worcestershire, salt, paprika, and hot pepper sauce; beat till smooth. Add garlic. Transfer to storage container; cover and chill.

Remove garlic before using. Makes 1⅓ cups (6 calories per tablespoon).

Diet Blue Cheese Dressing (opposite, center)

1 8-ounce carton plain yogurt
2 tablespoons crumbled blue
   cheese
2 teaspoons sugar
½ teaspoon celery seed
   Dash bottled hot pepper
   sauce

In a small mixer bowl combine yogurt, *half* the blue cheese, the sugar, celery seed, and hot pepper sauce. Beat with rotary beater till smooth. Stir in the remaining blue cheese. Transfer to storage container. Cover and chill. Makes 1 cup (13 calories per tablespoon).

Diet Salad Dressing

1 tablespoon all-purpose
   flour
1 tablespoon sugar
1 teaspoon dry mustard
½ teaspoon salt
   Dash cayenne
¾ cup skim milk
2 slightly beaten egg yolks
3 tablespoons vinegar

In saucepan combine flour, sugar, dry mustard, salt, and cayenne; stir in milk. Cook and stir till thick and bubbly. Gradually stir hot mixture into egg yolks. Return mixture to saucepan; cook and stir 2 minutes more. Place a piece of waxed paper over surface; cool 10 to 15 minutes. Remove waxed paper; stir in vinegar. Transfer to storage container; cover and chill. Makes ¾ cup (18 calories per tablespoon).

Diet Thousand Island Dressing (opposite, right)

½ cup Diet Salad Dressing
   (see recipe above)
1 tablespoon sliced green
   onion
1 tablespoon chopped green
   pepper
1 tablespoon catsup *or* chili
   sauce
1 tablespoon chopped pimiento
   (optional)
1 teaspoon prepared
   horseradish

In a small mixing bowl stir together *Diet Salad Dressing;* green onion; green pepper; catsup or chili sauce; pimiento, if desired; and horseradish. Transfer to storage container. Cover and chill. Makes ⅔ cup (16 calories per tablespoon).

Tomato Salad Dressing

1 8-ounce can tomato sauce
2 tablespoons tarragon
   vinegar
1 teaspoon worcestershire
   sauce
½ teaspoon salt
½ teaspoon dried dillweed
½ teaspoon dried basil,
   crushed
½ teaspoon onion juice

In screw-top jar combine tomato sauce, vinegar, worcestershire sauce, salt, dried dillweed, basil, and onion juice. Cover and shake to mix well. Chill thoroughly. Shake again just before serving. Makes 1 cup (4 calories per tablespoon).

Salad Toppers

Sprouting Mini Garden (pictured above, front to back: lentils, cress, and alfalfa)

Lentils
Alfalfa seed
Curly cress seed
Radish seed
Mustard seed
Mung beans
Garbanzos
Dried peas
Lima beans
Pinto beans

You can find some of these in the dried bean section of your supermarket. Shop a health food shop for the less common seeds. (Don't buy seeds that have been chemically treated for farming. Some treated seeds can be poisonous.)

In separate small bowls soak seeds in water (use four times as much water as seeds) till seeds swell to double in size, about 3 hours. Place three layers of paper toweling on divided plate; top with single layer of cheesecloth. Drain seeds; place in single layer atop cheesecloth. (Curly cress will develop a gelatinous coating; don't remove it.) Spray thoroughly with a fine water spray. (Towels should be wet but seeds shouldn't be standing in water.) Prick holes in a sheet of foil large enough to cover plate. Cover plate loosely with the foil. Place plate in a warm dark place. Spray with water 4 to 5 times a day at first, then 2 or 3 times daily after sprouts reach ¼ inch, keeping moist at all times. Sprouts grow in 2 to 3 days. Leaves appear on the third or fourth day. After sprouts appear, remove foil and set plates in sunny place for several hours to let the leaves turn green. Keep paper toweling wet. To harvest sprouts, snip off tops; use on tossed salads.

Garlic Croutons (pictured on page 81)

8 ½-inch-thick slices French
   bread
1 large clove garlic, halved
¼ cup salad oil
¼ cup butter *or* margarine
   softened

Rub both sides of bread slices with the cut clove of garlic; discard garlic. Gradually blend oil into softened butter or margarine; spread both sides of bread with oil-butter mixture. Cut bread into ½-inch cubes. Spread out on baking sheet. Bake in 300° oven for 20 to 25 minutes or till croutons are dry and crisp. Cool. Store in covered container in refrigerator. To serve, sprinkle over tossed salads. Makes 3 cups croutons.

Rye Croutons (pictured on page 81)

5 slices rye bread
3 tablespoons butter *or*
   margarine, softened

Brush both sides of rye bread slices with butter or margarine; cut bread into ½-inch cubes. Spread out on baking sheet. Bake in 300° oven for 20 to 25 minutes or till croutons are dry and crisp. Cool. Store in covered container in refrigerator. To serve, sprinkle over tossed salads. Makes 2 cups croutons.

Salad Garnishes

Radish Roses
Carrot Curls

To make Radish Roses, rinse radishes well; cut off tops and roots. Using tip of paring knife, cut 4 or 5 thin petal-shaped pieces around the outside of each radish (leave each petal attached at bottom).

To make Carrot Curls, rest peeled carrot on flat surface. Using vegetable peeler, shave thin wide strips the full length of carrot. Roll up; secure with wooden pick. Place vegetables in ice water to crispen.

Sprout Gardening in a Jar

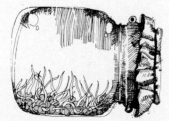

You can easily set up a sprout garden in the dark corner of a kitchen shelf. All you need is a quart jar, cheesecloth, and seeds (see suggested seeds in recipe at left). Wash and sort ½ cup of seeds, discarding damaged seeds. Soak seeds overnight in 2 cups water (seeds will swell to twice their size). Drain and rinse. Place ¼ cup of soaked seeds in each quart jar. Cover tops of jars with two layers of cheesecloth as shown; fasten each with rubber band or string. Place jars on their sides so seeds form shallow layer. Store in warm (68° to 75° F), dark place. Rinse seeds once daily in lukewarm water. Harvest sprouts in 3 to 5 days. You can eat the whole sprout: seed, root, stem, and outer hull. If you prefer to remove hulls, place sprouts in bowl; cover with water and stir vigorously, skimming away husks as they rise to the top. Drain. Pat dry with paper toweling. Sprinkle sprouts over tossed salads.

The Salad Kit

A salad is the result of an imaginative use of different foods. To see the results of a little free thinking, take a look at all the salad combinations you can create from the foods shown here.

Pasta Salad
Chilled macaroni, celery, olives, and green pepper.
Dressing
Mayonnaise with sugar and vinegar.

Bean Salad
Cooked or canned black-eyed peas, navy beans, lentils, and/or pinto beans, plus chopped green pepper, celery, onion, and pimiento.
Dressing
Oil, vinegar, and sugar.

Pantry Shelf Salad
Canned tuna, salmon, or chicken, chopped hard-cooked egg, chopped celery, and plenty of mayonnaise. Spread on toasted bread slices or pile into lettuce cups.

Artichoke Toss Salad
Chilled canned marinated artichokes, torn romaine, torn bibb, and tomato wedges.
Dressing
The marinade doubles as the dressing.

Spinach Salad
Torn raw spinach leaves, sliced mushrooms, crumbled bacon, and hard-cooked egg slices.
Dressing
Vinaigrette or Italian.

Potato Salad
Chilled cooked cubed potatoes, hard-cooked egg, chopped celery, radishes, onion, and olives.
Dressing
Mayonnaise with mustard or horseradish.

Mixed Vegetable Salad
Canned corn, green beans, and carrots, plus black olives and pimiento.
Dressing
Vinaigrette.

Citrus Salad
Grapefruit or orange sections, boston or bibb lettuce, sliced avocado.
Dressing
Yogurt with toasted sesame seed.

Sliced Tomato Salad
Sliced tomatoes on a platter surrounded with watercress leaves. Sprinkled with sliced green onion, chopped fresh basil, or parsley.
Dressing
Vinaigrette.

Oriental Salad
Bean sprouts, mushrooms, water chestnuts, scallions, and bok choy.
Dressing
Oil and vinegar plus soy sauce, sugar, garlic, and ginger.

Beet Salad
Canned or cooked beets, chopped onion, and anchovies.
Dressing
Italian.

Cucumber Salad
Sliced cucumber, sliced onion, salt, and pepper.
Dressing
Vinegar and sugar.

Gazpacho Salad
Chopped tomato, cucumber, green pepper, onion, and lots of snipped fresh parsley.
Dressing
Lemon juice, basil, garlic, and hot pepper sauce.

Mixed Green Salad
Escarole, romaine, boston, bibb, or all the above greens, plus snipped fresh herbs such as basil, chives, dill, or tarragon.
Dressing
Oil and vinegar.

Carrot Fruit Salad
Shredded carrot, crushed pineapple, and raisins, plus chopped nuts.
Dressing
Mayonnaise and sugar.

Curried Chicken Salad
Chicken cubes, grapes or orange sections, and peanuts.
Dressing
Mayonnaise and curry powder.

Guacamole Salad
Mixed salad greens, tomato wedges, and sliced onion rings.
Dressing
Mashed avocado blended with Italian dressing.

Marinated Vegetable Platter
Cook broccoli buds, cauliflowerets, carrot sticks, and zucchini slices. Drain. Pour on dressing; marinate overnight. Drain.
Dressing
Vinaigrette.

Hot Wilted Salad
Torn raw spinach leaves, leaf lettuce, or Swiss chard.
Dressing
Bacon drippings, chopped onion, vinegar, sugar, salt, and pepper; boil. Toss with greens.

Chef's Salad
Chilled sliced ham, beef, or chicken, mixed greens, cheese cubes, hard-cooked eggs.
Dressing
Russian.

Tropical Fruit Salad
Pineapple chunks, papaya slices, banana slices, strawberries, and kiwi fruit slices.
Dressing
Yogurt with lemon juice.

Seafood Salad
Torn salad greens, cold poached scallops, shrimp, cut-up lobster tails, scallions, chopped celery, and snipped parsley.
Dressing
Mayonnaise with chili sauce.

Mushroom Salad
Sliced fresh mushrooms and snipped chives.
Dressing
Vinaigrette.

Index